Cycling in
Scotland

Fergal MacErlean

Editor: Donna Wood
Designer: Phil Barfoot
Copy Editor: Helen Ridge
Proofreader: Judith Forshaw
Picture Researchers: Alice Earle (AA)
and Jonathan Bewley (Sustrans)
Image retouching and internal repro:
Sarah Montgomery and James Tims
Cartography provided by the Mapping Services
Department of AA Publishing from data provided by
Richard Sanders and Sustrans mapping team
Research and development by: Lindsey Ryle, Melissa
Henry, Julian Hunt, Katharine Taylor and John Lauder
Supplementary text: Nick Cotton
Production: Lorraine Taylor

Produced by AA Publishing

ISBN: 978-0-7495-7251-8

Published by AA Publishing (a trading name of
AA Media Limited, whose registered office is
Fanum House, Basing View, Basingstoke
RG21 4EA; registered number 06112600).

A04632

Free cycling permits are required on some British
Waterways canal towpaths. Visit www.waterscape.com
or call 0845 671 5530.

The National Cycle Network has been made possible
by the support and co-operation of hundreds of
organisations and thousands of individuals, including:
local authorities and councils, central governments
and their agencies, the National Lottery, landowners,
utility and statutory bodies, countryside and
regeneration bodies, the Landfill Communities Fund,
other voluntary organisations, charitable trusts and
foundations, the cycle trade and industry, corporate
sponsors, community organisations and Sustrans'
supporters. Sustrans would also like to extend thanks
to the thousands of volunteers who generously
contribute their time to looking after their local
sections of the Network.

Printed and bound in Dubai by Oriental Press
theAA.com/shop

Sustrans
2 Cathedral Square
College Green
Bristol BS1 5DD
www.sustrans.org.uk

Sustrans is a Registered Charity in the UK:
Number 326550 (England and Wales)
SC039263 (Scotland).

CONTENTS

Foreword by David Byrne 4

Introduction 6

National Cycle Network facts & figures 8

Locator map 9

Cycling with children 10

Hot tips & cool tricks 12

Bike maintenance 13

THE RIDES

 1 Edinburgh to Dalkeith 14

 2 Edinburgh to the Forth Road Bridge 18

 3 Balerno to Leith 22

 4 Musselburgh to Haddington 26

 5 Bathgate to Kirknewton 30

 6 Linlithgow to the Falkirk Wheel 34

 7 Galashiels to Dryburgh 38

 8 Strathclyde Loch to Chatelherault 42

 9 Paisley to Gourock 46

10 Bowling to the Falkirk Wheel 50

11 Bowling to Balloch 54

12 Paisley to Glengarnock 58

13 Ayr to Ardrossan 62

14 Kincardine to Limekilns 66

15 Alloa to Dunfermline 70

16 Aberfoyle to Callander 74

17 Callander to Killin 78

18 Perth to Dunkeld 82

19 Routes out of Dundee 86

20 The Caledonia Way 90

21 Barcaldine to Creagan 94

22 Lochgilphead to Crinan 98

23 Fort William to Laggan Locks 102

24 Aviemore to Carrbridge 106

25 Inverness to Dingwall 110

26 Aberdeen to Banchory 114

27 Dyce to Ellon 118

28 Cullen to Garmouth 122

Next steps 126

Join Sustrans 127

Acknowledgements 128

Foreword by **David Byrne,** musician and writer

I've seen people on biking holidays in the Highlands and on the west coast of Ireland. Masochists, if you ask me — pedalling in pelting rain against a fierce wind.

Why?

Granted, when the sun comes out it's glorious.

I myself have only biked around Glasgow and Edinburgh, and then usually just to get around — from a hotel in Leith up to a meeting in town, or to a lunch with friends, or to visit family in Glasgow or to find a place to rent some socks.

"Granted, when the sun comes out it's glorious"

For getting to and from music shows, clubs, museums and galleries, bikes are ideal... and I've never had one stolen, except in NY, though I did have one crushed by our own tour bus.

I've found that biking around for just a few hours a day, or even to and from work, helps keep me sane — so maybe this book could be your prescription for happier mental wellbeing?

Davl Byrne

ust a few hours
me sane

Ben Macdui viewed from Glen Lui

Edinburgh seen from Arthur's Seat

Mountain biking at Gleann an t-Slugain

Glasgow Science Centre

INTRODUCTION

It was in southern Scotland in 1839 that Kirkpatrick MacMillan – a blacksmith – created the first pedal-driven bicycle. It is little wonder, then, that the country that brought this most energy-efficient invention to the world should have some of the very best cycling on offer.

For families and adventurers alike, Scotland has a wealth of cycle routes to discover. And they're not all hilly, either – indeed, that resourceful blacksmith would have managed the majority of the rides in this guide on his iron-rimmed wooden wheels.

Hay bales at Campsie Fells

MacMillan set off on his inaugural ride from Thornhill, in Dumfriesshire, to Glasgow, a distance of some 60 miles (96.5km), where he promptly collided with a young girl in the city streets. The blacksmith was viewed as something of a menace but, in time, his invention gave pedal-powered freedom to the masses, of both sexes. In recent years, Scotland has produced some of the finest cyclists, with legends such as Graeme Obree and Chris Hoy among them. They, along with a growing number of ordinary commuters and leisure cyclists, are wise to the spread of opportunities north of the border.

One of the reasons why Scotland has some of the best cycling in the world is the ease with which you can escape the cities to explore the wild glens, scenic straths and long lochs. An impressive National Cycle Network system makes this not only possible but positively pleasant. For example, you can leave Waverley train station in Edinburgh's city centre and be pedalling seawards within minutes. Or, you could pack your saddle bags for an epic ride on the Lochs & Glens Route 7. This marvellous route runs all the way from Carlisle to Inverness, passing Glasgow, Loch Lomond and dozens of other points of interest. The famed Scottish hospitality and cycle-friendly initiatives, such as the Cyclists Welcome accommodation scheme, will keep your travel plans true.

This guide covers many excellent straightforward and non-taxing rides that will appeal not only to families and novice riders but to anyone with a yearning to steer their handlebars through this inspiring landscape,

Puffin on a grassy ledge

Vogrie Country Park

where history is never far away. On the ride from Oban through the peaceful and archaeologically rich Glen Lonan, for example, you cycle right by a 4m (13ft) high Bronze Age standing stone, which exudes an unmistakeable sense of the past.

Many of the routes detailed here follow disused railway lines – the legacy of Dr Beeching's report in the 1960s recommending the closure of lines and stations. These, of course, provide some of the very finest cycling – no steep gradients and totally car-free. Impressive viaducts are crossed, notably in West Lothian, where the towpath of the Union Canal leads 26m (85ft) above the River Avon, and the sense of space is heightened by the treetops below and the views out towards the Kingdom of Fife.

The National Cycle Network allows you to cycle through such inspiring landscapes with a minimum of fuss and traffic. Coordinated by sustainable transport charity Sustrans, it now extends for some 2,000 miles (3,200km) across Scotland, having increased from 500-odd miles (800km) in 1999. Major expansions are planned to encourage cycling for every type of journey.

Recently opened routes include a 3-mile (5km) section southwest of Ballachulish in Argyll. Sustrans hopes to finish the 33-mile (53km) route between Oban and Ballachulish by 2014. Completion is part of a wider plan to extend this traffic-free route north to Fort William, where the wonderful Caledonian Canal can be followed. It's another part of the plan to make cycling in Scotland even more attractive to all riders, young and old, big and small.

NATIONAL CYCLE NETWORK FACTS & FIGURES

Most of the routes featured here are part of the National Cycle Network. The aim of this book is to enable you to sample some of the highlights of the region on two wheels, but the rides given here are really just a taster as there are more than 13,000 miles of Network throughout the UK to explore. More than three-quarters of us live within two miles of one of the routes.

Over one million journeys a day are made on the National Cycle Network; for special trips like fun days out and holiday bike rides, but also the necessary everyday trips; taking people to school, to work, to the shops, to visit each other and to seek out green spaces. Half of these journeys are made on foot and half by bike, with urban traffic-free sections of the Network seeing the most usage.

The National Cycle Network is host to one of the UK's biggest collections of public art. Sculptures, benches, water fountains, viewing points and award-winning bridges enhance its pathways, making Sustrans one of the most prolific commissioners of public art in the UK.

The Network came into being following the award of the first-ever grant from the lottery, through the Millennium Commission, in 1995. Funding for the Network also came from bike retailers and manufacturers through the Bike

Hub, as well as local authorities and councils UK-wide, and Sustrans' many supporters. Over 2,500 volunteer Rangers give their time to Sustrans to assist in the maintenance of the National Cycle Network by adopting sections of route in communities throughout the UK. They remove glass and litter, cut back vegetation and try to ensure routes are well signed.

Developing and maintaining the National Cycle Network is just one of the ways in which Sustrans pursues its vision of a world in which people can choose to travel in ways that benefit their health and the environment.

We hope that you enjoy using this book to explore the paths and cycleways of the National Cycle Network and we would like to thank the many hundreds of organisations who have worked with Sustrans to develop the walking and cycling routes, including every local authority and council in the UK.

MAP LEGEND

Traffic Free/On Road route	Ride Start or Finish Point	National Cycle Network (Traffic Free)	National Cycle Network (On Road)

Symbol	Item	Symbol	Item	Symbol	Item
PH	AA recommended pub		Farm or animal centre		Theme park
	Abbey, cathedral or priory		Garden	i	Tourist Information Centre
	Abbey, cathedral or priory in ruins		Hill-fort		Viewpoint
	Aquarium		Historic house	V	Visitor or heritage centre
	Aqueduct or viaduct		Industrial attraction		World Heritage Site (UNESCO)
	Arboretum		Marina		Zoo or wildlife collection
×	Battle site		Monument		AA golf course
	Bird Reserve (RSPB)	M	Museum or gallery		Stadium
	Cadw (Welsh Heritage) site		National Nature Reserve:		Indoor Arena
△	Campsite		England, Scotland, Wales		Tennis
	Caravan site		Local nature reserve		Horse racing
	Caravan & campsite		National Trust property		Rugby Union
	Castle		National Trust for Scotland property		Football
	Cave		Picnic site		Athletics
	Country park		Roman remains		Motorsports
	English Heritage site		Steam railway		County cricket

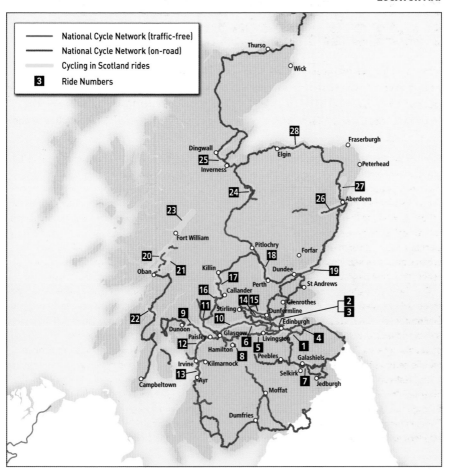

National Cycle Network (traffic-free)
National Cycle Network (on-road)
Cycling in Scotland rides
3 Ride Numbers

KEY TO LOCATOR MAP

1	Edinburgh to Dalkeith	**15**	Alloa to Dunfermline
2	Edinburgh to the Forth Road Bridge	**16**	Aberfoyle to Callander
3	Balerno to Leith	**17**	Callander to Killin
4	Musselburgh to Haddington	**18**	Perth to Dunkeld
5	Bathgate to Kirknewton	**19**	Routes out of Dundee
6	Linlithgow to the Falkirk Wheel	**20**	The Caledonia Way
7	Galashiels to Dryburgh	**21**	Barcaldine to Creagan
8	Strathclyde Loch to Chatelherault	**22**	Lochgilphead to Crinan
9	Paisley to Gourock	**23**	Fort William to Laggan Locks
10	Bowling to the Falkirk Wheel	**24**	Aviemore to Carrbridge
11	Bowling to Balloch	**25**	Inverness to Dingwall
12	Paisley to Glengarnock	**26**	Aberdeen to Banchory
13	Ayr to Ardrossan	**27**	Dyce to Ellon
14	Kincardine to Limekilns	**28**	Cullen to Garmouth

CYCLING WITH CHILDREN

Kids love bikes and love to ride. Cycling helps them to grow up fit, healthy and independent, and introduces them to the wider world and the adventure it holds.

TOP TIPS FOR FAMILY BIKE RIDES:

- Take along snacks, drinks and treats to keep their energy and spirit levels up.
- Don't be too ambitious. It's much better that everyone wants to go out again, than all coming home exhausted, tearful and permanently put off cycling.
- Plan your trip around interesting stops and sights along the way. Don't make journey times any longer than children are happy to sit and play at home.
- Even on a fine day, take extra clothes and waterproofs – just in case. Check that trousers and laces can't get caught in the chain when pedalling along.
- Wrap up toddlers. When a young child is on the back of a bike, they won't be generating heat like the person doing all the pedalling!
- Be careful not to pinch their skin when putting their helmet on. It's easily done and often ends in tears. Just place your forefinger between the clip and the chin.
- Ride in a line with the children in the middle of the adults. If there's only one of you, the adult should be at the rear, keeping an eye on all the children in front. Take special care at road junctions.
- Check that children's bikes are ready to ride. Do the brakes and gears work? Is the saddle the right height? Are the tyres pumped up?
- Carry some sticking plasters and antiseptic wipes – kids are far more likely to fall off and graze arms, hands or knees.
- Take a camera to record the trip – memories are made of this.

TRANSPORTING YOUNG CHILDREN ON TWO WHEELS

It's now easier than ever for you to ride your bike with young children.

- **Child seats:** *6 months to five years (one child).* Once a baby can support its own head (usually at 6–12 months) they can be carried in a child seat. Seats are fitted mainly to the rear of the bike.
- **Trailers:** babies to five years *(up to two children).* Young babies can be strapped into their car seat and carried in a trailer, and older children can be strapped in and protected from the wind and rain.
- **Tag-along trailer bikes:** *approx four to nine years.* Tag-alongs (the back half of a child's bike attached to the back of an adult one) allow a child to be towed while they either add some of their own pedal power or just freewheel and enjoy the ride.
- **Tow bar:** *approx four to eight years.* A tow bar converts a standard child's bike to a trailer bike by lifting their front wheel from the ground to prevent them from steering, while enabling them to pedal independently. When you reach a safe place, the tow bar can be detached and the child's bike freed.

TEACHING YOUR CHILD TO RIDE

There are lots of ways for children to develop and gain cycling confidence before they head out on their own.

- **Tricycles or trikes:** available for children from ten months to five years old. They have pedals so kids have all the fun of getting around under their own steam.
- **Balance bikes:** are like normal bikes but without the pedals. This means children learn to balance, steer and gain confidence on two wheels while being able to place their feet firmly and safely on the ground.

- **Training wheels:** stabilisers give support to the rear of the bike and are the easiest way to learn to ride but potentially the slowest.

BUYING THE RIGHT BIKE FOR YOUR CHILD

Every child develops differently and they may be ready to learn to ride between the ages of three and seven. When children do progress to their own bike, emphasising the fun aspect will help them take the tumbles in their stride. Encouragement and praise are important to help them persevere.

Children's bikes generally fall into age categories based on the average size of a child of a specific age. There are no hard and fast rules, as long as your child isn't stretched and can reach the brakes safely and change gear easily. It's important to buy your child a bike that fits them rather than one they can grow into. Ask your local bike shop for advice and take your child along to try out different makes and sizes.

To find a specialist cycle retailer near you visit www.thecyclingexperts.co.uk

HOT TIPS & COOL TRICKS...

WHAT TO WEAR

For most of the rides featured in this book you do not need any special clothing or footwear. Shoes that are suitable for walking are also fine for cycling. Looser-fitting trousers allow your legs to move more freely, while tops with zips let you regulate your temperature. In cold weather, take gloves and a warm hat; it's also a good idea to pack a waterproof. If you are likely to be out at dusk, take a bright reflective top. If you start to cycle regularly, you may want to invest in some specialist equipment for longer rides, especially padded shorts and gloves.

WHAT TO TAKE

For a short ride, the minimum you will need is a pump and a small tool bag with a puncture repair kit, just in case. However, it is worth considering the following: water bottle, spare inner tube, 'multi-tool' (available from cycle shops), lock, money, sunglasses, lightweight waterproof (some pack down as small as a tennis ball), energy bars, map, camera and a spare top in case it cools down or to keep you warm when you stop for refreshments.

HOW TO TAKE IT

Rucksacks are fine for light loads but can make your back hot and sweaty. For heavier loads and for longer or more regular journeys, you are better off with panniers that attach to a bike rack.

BIKE ACCESSORIES

You may also want to invest in a helmet. A helmet will not prevent accidents from happening but can provide protection if you do fall off your bike. They are particularly recommended for young children. Ultimately, wearing a helmet is a question of individual choice and parents need to make that choice for their children.

A bell is a must for considerate cyclists. A friendly tinkle warns that you are approaching, but never assume others can hear you.

LOCKING YOUR BIKE

Unless you are sitting right next to your bike when you stop for refreshments, it is worth locking it, preferably to something immovable like a post, fence or railings (or a bike stand, of course). If nothing else, lock it to a companion's bike. Bike theft is more common in towns and cities, and if you regularly leave your bike on the streets, it is important to invest in a good-quality lock and to lock and leave your bike in a busy, well-lit location.

GETTING TO THE START OF A RIDE

The best rides are often those that you can do right from your doorstep, maximizing time on your bike and reducing travelling time. If you need to travel to the start of the ride, have you thought about catching a train?

FINDING OUT MORE – WWW.SUSTRANS.ORG.UK

Use the Sustrans website to find out where you can cycle to from home or while you are away on holiday, and browse through a whole host of other useful information.
Visit www.sustrans.org.uk

MAKING THE MOST OF YOUR BIKE

Making a few simple adjustments to your bike will make your ride more enjoyable and comfortable:

- **Saddle height:** raise or lower it so that you have good contact with your pedals (to make the most of your leg power) and so that you can always put a reassuring foot on the ground.
- **Saddle position:** getting the saddle in the right place will help you get the most from your pedal power without straining your body.
- **Handlebars:** well-positioned handlebars are crucial for your comfort and important for control of your steering and brakes.

...BIKE MAINTENANCE

Like any machine, a bike will work better and last longer if you care for it properly. Get in the habit of checking your bike regularly – simple checks and maintenance can help you have hassle-free riding and avoid repairs.

- **Tools:** there are specialist tools for specific tasks, but all you need to get started are: a pump, an old toothbrush, lubricants and grease, cleaning rags, a puncture repair kit, tyre levers, allen keys, screwdrivers and spanners.

REGULAR CHECKS

- **Every week:** Check tyres, brakes, lights, handlebars and seat are in good order and tightly secured.
- **Every month:** Wipe clean and lubricate chain with chain oil.
  Wipe the dirt from wheels.
  Check tread on tyres.
  Check brake pads.
  Check gear and brake cables and make sure that gears are changing smoothly.
- **Every year:** Take your bike to an experienced mechanic for a thorough service.
- **Tip:** If in doubt, leave it to the professionals. Bike mechanics are much more affordable than car mechanics, and some will even collect the bike from your home and return it to you when all the work is done.

FIXING A PUNCTURE

Punctures don't happen often and are easy to fix yourself. If you don't fancy repairing a puncture on your journey, carry a spare inner tube and a pump so you can change the tube, then fix the puncture when you get home. If you don't mind repairing punctures when they happen, make sure you carry your repair kit and pump with you at all times. All puncture repair kits have full instructions with easy-to-follow pictures.

Alternatively, if you don't want to get your hands dirty, just visit your local bike shop and they will fix the puncture for you.

Regular checks and inspections

Mending a puncture: easy peasy

Yearly professional checks and servicing

A CAPITAL RIDE – EDINBURGH TO DALKEITH

Edinburgh is a very cycle-friendly city, as this route, which starts right in the heart of the capital, demonstrates. Within minutes of alighting at Waverley train station you can be pedalling along to your heart's content by the dramatic form of Arthur's Seat. This rock formation, which rises from Holyrood Park, is an ancient volcano – a reminder of a time when Scotland's geology was explosive.

Following National Route 1, from Edinburgh to Dalkeith, this excellent route leads into Midlothian along a cyclepath that is almost entirely traffic-free. A particularly memorable section is encountered early on where the route passes through a 320m (1,050ft) long tunnel, part of the former Innocent Railway. Built in 1831, the railway – one of the earliest in Scotland – got its unusual name from originally being horse-drawn; at the time, steam engines were notorious for causing casualties.

Roll on to follow a pretty path by the River Esk to the south of Musselburgh. Here you could take a pleasant detour to the seaside town for a paddle. Another excellent railway path is followed to Dalkeith, where you can enjoy the sylvan delights of Dalkeith Country Estate. Once rested, there's the option of returning to Musselburgh to catch a train back to the centre of Edinburgh.

ROUTE INFORMATION

National Route: 1
Start: Waverley train station, Edinburgh.
Finish: Musselburgh Road, Dalkeith.
Distance: 13 miles (21km).
Grade: Easy.
Surface: Tarmac.
Hills: Almost all flat, except for final, walkable hill on the approach to Dalkeith.

YOUNG & INEXPERIENCED CYCLISTS

Traffic-free cyclepaths for most of the route. Exceptions are the Edinburgh city centre section, and short stretches in Brunstane, Newcraighall, Musselburgh and Whitecraig, which could all be easily walked by inexperienced cyclists.

REFRESHMENTS

- A number of options at urban centres en route.
- Di Rollo, Musselburgh (ice cream parlour).
- Lucas, Musselburgh (ice cream parlour).
- Lots of choice in Dalkeith.

THINGS TO SEE & DO

- **National Museum of Scotland:** includes ancient Viking brooches, Pictish stones, Lewis chessmen and beautiful silverwork such as ornate quaichs and Queen Mary's clarsach (harp). More modern exhibits include Dolly the sheep, the first cloned mammal; 0300 123 6789; www.nms.ac.uk
- **Arthur's Seat, Holyrood Park:** enjoy a hike up this extinct volcano for views that will really take your breath away; from the top you can see across to Fife, down to Musselburgh and beyond, along the East Lothian coast; http://walking.visitscotland.com
- **Craigmillar Castle, Craigmillar:** striking and well-preserved medieval castle linked to the intriguing story of Mary Queen of Scots; it boasts one of the oldest tower houses in Scotland and has an impressive great hall; 0131 661 4445; www.historic-scotland.gov.uk
- **Musselburgh Links, Balcarres Road:** the oldest playing golf course in the world, with an impressive range of memorabilia for sale; 0131 665 5438; www.musselburgholdlinks.co.uk

View towards Arthur's Seat from Edinburgh Castle

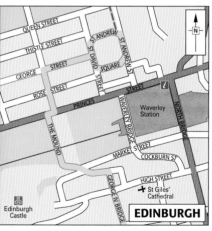

EDINBURGH

- **Dalkeith Country Estate:** picturesque 500-acre woodland with a network of walking trails (many of which can be cycled), ancient oak specimens, an extensive and exciting children's playground, and a tearoom; admission charges for cyclists riding through apply during standard opening hours; 0131 654 1666; www.dalkeithcountryestate.com

TRAIN STATIONS

Edinburgh Waverley; Brunstane; Newcraighall; Musselburgh.

BIKE HIRE
- Biketrax, Edinburgh: 0131 228 6633; www.biketrax.co.uk
- Cycle Scotland, Edinburgh: 0131 556 5560; www.cyclescotland.co.uk
- Leith Cycle Co, Leith: 0131 467 7775; www.leithcycleco.com

FURTHER INFORMATION
- To view or print National Cycle Network routes, visit www.sustrans.org.uk
- Maps for this area are available to buy from www.sustransshop.co.uk
- For more information on routes in Scotland, visit www.routes2ride.org.uk/scotland
- Edinburgh Tourist Information: 0845 225 5121; 0131 625 8625; www.edinburgh.org
- Scotland Tourist Information: 0845 225 5121; 0131 625 8625; www.visitscotland.com

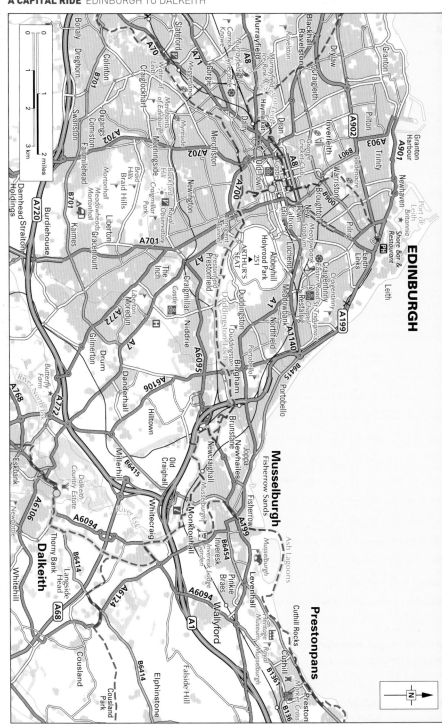

The romantic ruins of Craigmillar Castle

ROUTE DESCRIPTION

See the inset map on page 15 for directions from Waverley station to Route 1 (highlighted). Follow Route 1 south to Meadow Park and then east towards Holyrood Park. From St Leonard's Lane, near Holyrood Park, follow Route 1 downhill, through the Innocent Railway tunnel. Continue on the old railway line, following Route 1 signs for Dalkeith across two busy roads to reach a flyover (with steps) across the tracks by Brunstane station. A section on-road continues for 0.5 mile (0.8km), followed by a 0.25-mile (0.4m) stretch along the main road through Newcraighall. A newly built traffic-free cyclepath then leads to Queen Margaret's University College by Musselburgh train station.

Pedal on through residential streets, cross the river and turn right onto a path by the River Esk, which leads to Whitecraig. At the far edge of Whitecraig, cross the road to follow another old railway line leading to the edge of Dalkeith, where a final shared-use pavement leads uphill to the town centre, passing Dalkeith Country Estate. When the construction begins on the Borders Railway line, Route 1 will be realigned through Dalkeith – follow the signs.

NEARBY CYCLE ROUTES

The Edinburgh to Dalkeith trail is part of the

Innocent Railway tunnel

Musselburgh harbour

Coast & Castles Route (National Route 1) which runs for 368 miles (592km) from Newcastle to Aberdeen. This popular route passes areas of historic interest and beautiful coastline.

Many of the estate tracks at Dalkeith Country Estate are suitable for cyclists, providing some lovely family-friendly rides.

EDINBURGH TO THE FORTH ROAD BRIDGE

Edinburgh's architectural delights are far too numerous to list here but, from a cycling perspective, riding across the Forth Road Bridge is one of the most extraordinary experiences to be had in Scotland. You cross from South Queensferry to North Queensferry in complete traffic-free safety along the cycle lanes that run either side of the bridge, hundreds of feet above the waters of the Firth of Forth, with views to the east of the magnificent Forth Rail Bridge (the one where, as the saying goes, they start painting at one end the moment they have stopped at the other!)

The route starts from Haymarket in central Edinburgh, using a railway path to leave the city to the northwest, passing close by 16th-century Lauriston Castle. Just beyond Cramond Brig, you have a choice of taking roads to Dalmeny or a more leisurely ride along the coastline of the Firth of Forth, which passes Dalmeny House, built in 1817 by the Earl of Rosebery in the Gothic Revival style.

Queensferry was named after Queen Margaret, who used the ferry to cross the Forth in the 11th century.

ROUTE INFORMATION
National Routes: 1, 76
Start: Haymarket train station, Edinburgh.
Finish: North end of the Forth Road Bridge, North Queensferry.
Distance: 11 miles (17.5km).
Alternative coastal route: 13 miles (21km).
Grade: Easy to moderate.
Surface: Tarmac.
Hills: Rolling.

YOUNG & INEXPERIENCED CYCLISTS

At the time of writing, there are proposed changes to National Route 1 in the Haymarket area of Edinburgh, and the route will use either quiet residential streets or a busy road from Haymarket train station until the start of the railway path at Roseburn. Care should be taken on the roads and crossings in Dalmeny. There are road sections in South

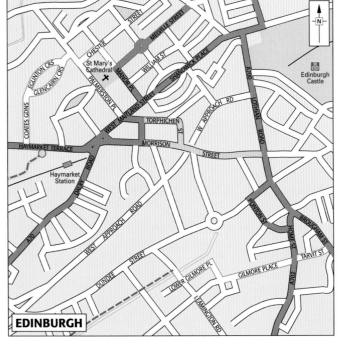

EDINBURGH

Forth Rail Bridge in the evening light

Queensferry and from the bridge to North Queensferry. The most exciting section for children is the crossing of the Forth Road Bridge itself, with its traffic-free cycle lanes.

REFRESHMENTS
- Cramond Brig pub, Cramond.
- Tearoom in Dalmeny House, open Sunday, Monday and Tuesday afternoons in July and August.
- The Forth Bridges Hotel, South Queensferry.
- Various choices in South Queensferry village.
- Albert Hotel, Ferrybridge Hotel or Post Office Cafe in North Queensferry.

THINGS TO SEE & DO
- **Edinburgh Castle:** iconic feature of Edinburgh, perched on an extinct volcano; 0131 225 9846; www.edinburghcastle.gov.uk
- **National Gallery of Scotland:** 0131 624 6336; www.nationalgalleries.org
- **Scottish National Gallery of Modern Art:** 0131 624 6336; www.nationalgalleries.org
- **Scottish National Portrait Gallery:** 0131 624 6336; www.nationalgalleries.org
- **Royal Botanic Garden:** established in 1670, 70 acres of landscaped gardens, 1 mile (1.6km) from the city centre; 0131 552 7171; www.rbge.org.uk

- **Palace of Holyroodhouse:** official residence in Scotland of Her Majesty The Queen, situated at the end of the Royal Mile; 0131 556 5100; www.royalcollection.org.uk
- **Georgian House:** restored Edinburgh town house filled with Georgian artefacts; 0844 493 2117; www.nts.org.uk
- **Lauriston Castle:** 16th-century tower house with 19th-century Jacobean-style additions; 0131 336 2060; www.museumsgalleriesscotland.org.uk
- **Cramond Fort:** site of Roman fort; www.undiscoveredscotland.co.uk
- **Deep Sea World, North Queensferry:** includes the UK's longest underwater viewing tunnel, coral reefs, sharks and seal sanctuary; 01383 411880; www.deepseaworld.com

TRAIN STATIONS
Edinburgh Waverley; Edinburgh Haymarket; South Gyle; Dalmeny; North Queensferry.

BIKE HIRE
- **Bike Trax, Edinburgh:** 0131 228 6633; www.biketrax.co.uk
- **Cycle Scotland, Edinburgh:** 0131 556 5560; www.cyclescotland.co.uk
- **Leith Cycle Co, Leith:** 0131 467 7775; www.leithcycleco.com

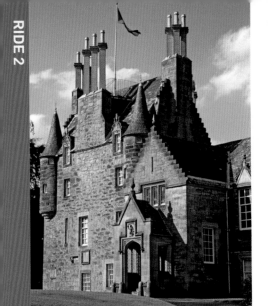

Lauriston Castle,
Edinburgh

along the coastline of the Firth of Forth, past Dalmeny House and along the High Street of historic South Queensferry, before a short climb leads from Hopetoun Road up to the bridge, where you rejoin Route 1.

After crossing the bridge, you have the option of going into North Queensferry using a road section from the cycle path down to the village for refreshments, visiting Deep Sea World and taking a train back to Edinburgh across the Forth Rail Bridge. (From the centre of the old village of North Queensferry, there's a steep climb back up to the station.)

If you decide to cycle back to Edinburgh, follow the signs for Route 1 from the south side of the Forth Road Bridge or take the ramp down from the bridge to follow Route 76 through South Queensferry and around the Dalmeny Estate. You rejoin Route 1 back to Edinburgh at Cramond Bridge.

NEARBY CYCLE ROUTES

National Route 75, the Clyde to Forth Cycle Route, runs across Scotland, from Gourock to Leith. National Route 754 uses the towpaths of the Union and Forth & Clyde Canals, from Bowling on the Clyde to Fountainbridge in Edinburgh.

National Route 1 northbound (Coast & Castles North) connects Edinburgh with St Andrews and Dundee, and continues along the coast to Aberdeen and Inverness, eventually ending in Shetland. National Route 1 southbound is the Coast & Castles South Route, which runs from Edinburgh to Dalkeith, then south through the Scottish Borders to Berwick-upon-Tweed, following the coast to Newcastle upon Tyne.

National Route 76 runs from Edinburgh to Stirling around both sides of the Forth Estuary, and to Berwick-upon-Tweed via Dunbar.

There are many traffic-free trails in or near Edinburgh, such as the Innocent Railway Path, the Water of Leith, the Union Canal, and the North Edinburgh Railway Paths.

FURTHER INFORMATION

- To view or print National Cycle Network routes, visit www.sustrans.org.uk
- Maps for this area are available to buy from www.sustransshop.co.uk
- For more information on routes in Scotland, visit www.routes2ride.org.uk/scotland
- Edinburgh Tourist Information: 0845 225 5121; 0131 625 8625; www.edinburgh.org
- Scotland Tourist Information: 0845 225 5121; 0131 625 8625; www.visitscotland.com

ROUTE DESCRIPTION

The ride out from Haymarket train station in central Edinburgh uses a mixture of cyclepaths, railway paths and quiet roads through Davidson's Mains, Barnton and across the River Almond on the lovely old Cramond Bridge. Just past here, you come to the junction of National Routes 1 and 76.

Route 1 uses cycle tracks alongside roads and a quiet road to Dalmeny. It then takes quiet streets and cyclepaths through South Queensferry, to cross the Forth Road Bridge (Route 1 uses the east cycle lane).

Alternatively, Route 76 takes a longer route

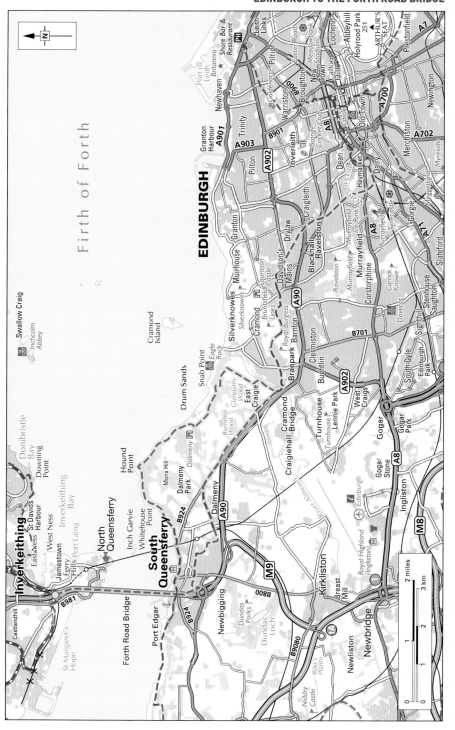

WATER OF LEITH – BALERNO TO LEITH

This gradually downhill cycle route, on National Route 75 alongside the Water of Leith and the Union Canal, has a great sense of progression. Passing numerous points of interest, it leads, pleasingly, through the heart of Scotland's capital.

The Water of Leith springs from the Pentland Hills and carves a course through Edinburgh to the sea at Leith. It has been of enormous importance to the city, driving dozens of waterwheels along its length, which produced paper, flour, timber, cloth and even spices and snuff.

The first part of the route, from Balerno to Slateford, follows the upper section of the river, passing the attractive wooded Colinton. Further on, the route joins the Union Canal. A highlight of the trip is where the canal crosses the 18m (59ft) high Slateford Aqueduct. The towpath leads on, past gaily-coloured barges, to end at Edinburgh Quay. In times past, goods for the city would have been unloaded near here.

Route 75 continues through the grassy Meadows, across the historic Royal Mile, and down through the New Town to Broughton, where it returns to the Water of Leith. An easy run now leads along a dedicated cyclepath to The Shore at Leith, where you can watch the river spill into the sea.

ROUTE INFORMATION

National Route: 75
Start: Balerno High School, Balerno.
Finish: The Shore, Leith.
Distance: 12 miles (19.5km).
Grade: Easy.

Edinburgh Castle

Surface: Gravel and tarmac.
Hills: Gradual descent from Balerno, flat along the canal, some steep downhill sections in the city centre.

YOUNG & INEXPERIENCED CYCLISTS

Novices and children may prefer to walk their bikes along the pavement in the Edinburgh city centre section.

REFRESHMENTS

- Scott of Juniper Green (deli).
- Water of Leith Visitor Centre, Slateford.
- Upper Crust Cafe, Balerno.
- Plenty of choice in Edinburgh and at the end of the ride in Leith.

THINGS TO SEE & DO

- Water of Leith Visitor Centre, Slateford: well-presented information on the river's rich historical past and present-day flora and fauna; 0131 455 7367; www.waterofleith.org.uk
- Edinburgh Castle: perched on an extinct volcano, this fortress is a powerful national symbol and part of Edinburgh's World

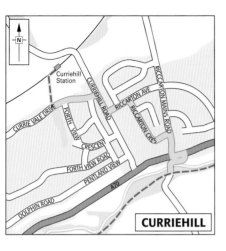

CURRIEHILL

The Meadows in Edinburgh

Wood carving at Balerno

Heritage Site; 0131 225 9846; www.edinburghcastle.gov.uk
- **Royal Botanic Garden, Edinburgh:** delightful gardens with noteworthy Himalayan and glasshouse collections; cyclists very welcome; 0131 552 7171; www.rbge.org.uk
- **Royal Yacht Britannia, Ocean Terminal, Leith:** once the floating royal residence for the Queen and the Royal Family, and now a five-star tourist attraction; 0131 555 5566; www.royalyachtbritannia.co.uk

TRAIN STATIONS
Curriehill; Kingsknowe; Slateford; Waverley.

BIKE HIRE
- **Biketrax, Edinburgh:** 0131 228 6633; www.biketrax.co.uk
- **Cycle Scotland, Edinburgh:** 0131 556 5560; www.cyclescotland.co.uk
- **Leith Cycle Co, Leith:** 0131 467 7775; www.leithcycleco.com

FURTHER INFORMATION
- To view or print National Cycle Network routes, visit www.sustrans.org.uk
- Maps for this area are available to buy from www.sustransshop.co.uk
- For further information on routes in Scotland, visit www.routes2ride.org.uk/scotland
- **Edinburgh Tourist Information:** 0845 225 5121; 0131 625 8625; www.edinburgh.org
- **Scotland Tourist Information:** 0845 225 5121; 0131 625 8625; www.visitscotland.com

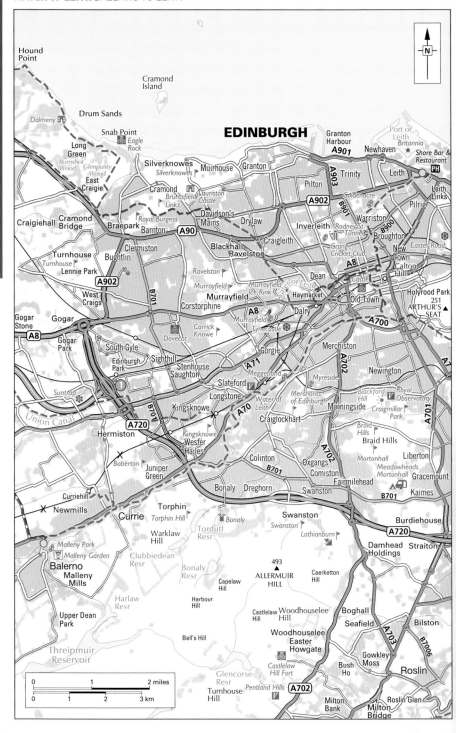

ROUTE DESCRIPTION

The ride begins at Balerno High School, Bridge Road, which can be reached via quiet roads from the stations at Curriehill or Kirknewton, and follows National Route 75 throughout. The initial section is shared with the Water of Leith Walkway. Further on it crosses, and joins, the Union Canal towpath and heads east for Edinburgh (to the west is a link to Kingsknowe train station).

At the canal end at Edinburgh Quay, after an on-road section, Route 75 leads to a quiet cyclepath through The Meadows. A longer on-road section then goes through the heart of the city, by Edinburgh Castle, St Andrew Square and the eastern part of the New Town. The final leg of Route 75 runs through another railway tunnel to join the traffic-free cyclepath, which runs parallel to the Water of Leith, to reach The Shore at Leith.

NEARBY CYCLE ROUTES

This Water of Leith trail is part of the longer Clyde to Forth Route (National Route 75) which connects Leith with Edinburgh and extends west to Glasgow, Gourock and the Cowal Peninsula. Following the reopening of the Airdrie to Bathgate railway, a new traffic-free path has been completed for Route 75 between Bathgate and Plains. A shared-use path is being constructed alongside the A89 from Plains to Drumgelloch in east Airdrie. Part of the city centre section is shared with National Route 1. Route 1 connects Dover with the Shetland Islands. An attractive section (Coast & Castles) connects Newcastle to Aberdeen.

The Water of Leith Walkway is a delightful shared-use path that follows the river from Balerno to Leith. The surface is variable with some muddy sections and flights of steps, though there are no steps on the sections used by Route 75.

The Union Canal extends from Edinburgh Quay to the Falkirk Wheel (National Route 754). At the Falkirk Wheel it joins the Forth & Clyde Canal, which leads west to Bowling. The canal towpaths provide excellent cycling for all the family. Sustrans is working with British Waterways to improve the surface and remove barriers along the towpaths.

Gentle traffic-free cycling

COASTING ALONG – MUSSELBURGH TO HADDINGTON

The huge Firth of Forth is seen in all its glory on this section of the Round the Forth Route (National Route 76). It makes for a great ride: much of it uses traffic-free cyclepaths and it's wonderfully flat, too! After a link from Musselburgh train station on National Route 1, turn left to join Route 76 along a willow-lined stretch by the River Esk.

You soon reach Musselburgh Racecourse and historic Musselburgh Links – golf was played here as far back as 1672, although Mary Queen of Scots might have enjoyed a game considerably earlier, in 1567. The Old Links at Musselburgh was originally a seven-hole course, with another added in 1838; the full nine holes came into play in 1870. A little further on you will pass the grey lagoons of a bird sanctuary, made from reclaimed land composed of ash from Cockenzie power station.

Next, the route passes close by Prestongrange Museum, where you can detour to learn about the myriad previous activities at this important Industrial Revolution site.

Enjoy the views and sea air as you pedal on to Longniddry along an old railway line that leads to the attractive market town of Haddington. From Haddington, you can retrace your tyre tracks to Longniddry station, a distance of 4.5 miles (7km), to catch a train.

ROUTE INFORMATION
National Routes: 1, 76
Start: Musselburgh train station.
Finish: Haddington town centre.
Distance: 17 miles (27.5km).
Grade: Easy.
Surface: Tarmac; short hard-core section by Musselburgh ash lagoons; fine gravel on railway path.
Hills: None.

YOUNG & INEXPERIENCED CYCLISTS
The majority of the route follows traffic-free cyclepaths. Care must be taken on the on-road sections.

REFRESHMENTS
• Di Rollo, Musselburgh (ice cream parlour).
• Lucas, Musselburgh (ice cream parlour).
• Variety of options in Prestonpans, Cockenzie, Longniddry and Haddington.

THINGS TO SEE & DO
• **Musselburgh Links, Balcarres Road:** the oldest playing golf course in the world, with an impressive range of memorabilia for sale; 0131 665 5438; www.musselburgholdlinks.co.uk
• **Prestongrange Industrial Heritage Museum, Morrison's Haven, Prestonpans:** Prestongrange is a site of major importance in the story of Scotland's Industrial Revolution; remnants of its former industries and restored engines can be seen; 0131 653 2904; www.prestongrange.org
• **Seton Collegiate Church, near Seton:** set in wooded surroundings close to the cyclepath, this is one of the finest medieval collegiate churches surviving in Scotland; 01875 813334; www.historic-scotland.gov.uk
• **St Martin's Kirk, Haddington:** on the eastern outskirts of the town, this ruined nave is all that remains of a once splendid Romanesque church; 0131 668 8600; www.historic-scotland.gov.uk

TRAIN STATIONS
Musselburgh; Wallyford; Prestonpans; Longniddry.

Haddington's
Nungate Bridge

BIKE HIRE
- **Biketrax, Edinburgh:** 0131 228 6633; www.biketrax.co.uk
- **Cycle Scotland, Edinburgh:** 0131 556 5560; www.cyclescotland.co.uk
- **Leith Cycle Co, Leith:** 0131 467 7775; www.leithcycleco.com

FURTHER INFORMATION
- To view or print National Cycle Network routes, visit www.sustrans.org.uk
- Maps for this area are available to buy from www.sustransshop.co.uk
- For further information on routes in Scotland, visit www.routes2ride.org.uk/scotland
- **North Berwick Tourist Information:** 01620 892197; www.edinburgh.org

- **Scotland Tourist Information:** 0845 225 5121; 0131 625 8625; www.visitscotland.com

ROUTE DESCRIPTION
More than half this new route is traffic-free, providing a pleasant way to travel along a scenic stretch of coast. Starting from Musselburgh train station, follow National Route 1 signs east for Dalkeith. A stretch through a quiet residential area and a section of traffic-free cyclepath lead to an intersection with Route 76 after crossing the River Esk.

Turn left down the riverside cyclepath. Further on, a quiet on-road section leads to the shore, passing Musselburgh's racecourse and historic golf course. The route follows a coastal path, shared with the John Muir Way, alongside ash lagoons. The first part of this shore path is

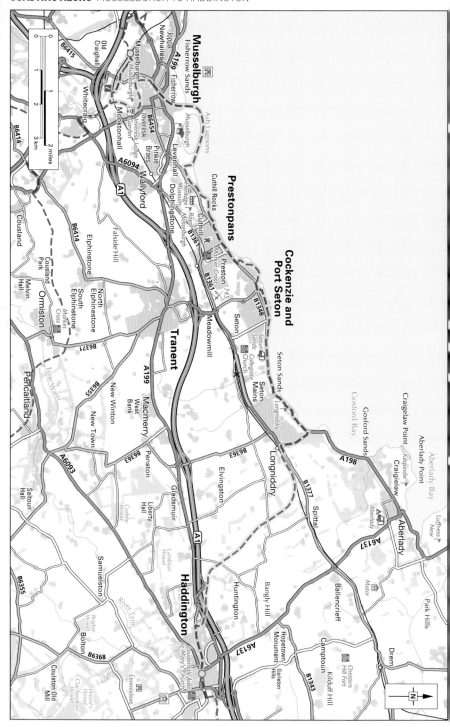

St Martin's Kirk, Haddington

a rough hard-core road but later it is well surfaced. It continues to Prestonpans, with an on-road section leading through the pleasant seaside town.

From Cockenzie to Seton Sands there is a shared-use pavement, then an on-road section to Longniddry train station. Turn left at the roundabout onto the B1377 to Drem and look for signs on the right to the cyclepath along an old railway line, which takes you under the A1 to the outskirts of Haddington. An on-road section leads into the town.

NEARBY CYCLE ROUTES

The Musselburgh to Haddington trail is part of the Round the Forth Route (National Route 76), which currently follows the coast from Berwick-upon-Tweed to Edinburgh, Stirling and Kirkcaldy. In time, it will continue round the East Neuk of Fife to St Andrews. The Coast & Castles Route (National Route 1) is followed from Musselburgh train station to the River Esk. The Coast & Castles Route runs from Newcastle to Aberdeen, passing many areas of historic interest. The Pencaitland Railway Path (signed Route 196) is a superb traffic-free route

Musselburgh Golf Links

through the East Lothian countryside. The 7-mile (11km) unsurfaced path can be accessed off Route 1, south of Whitecraig, and from the riverside path running to the south of Haddington.

A WEST LOTHIAN EXCURSION – BATHGATE TO KIRKNEWTON

Bog lovers will find plenty of interest on this outing through West Lothian. The first mire – the Bogburn Flood Lagoons – is protected as a reserve, where more than 500 species have been recorded. These include lichens, butterflies, moths, sawflies and stoneflies. The area is also rich in reed, sedge, horsetail and meadowsweet beds, which are a joy to see in the spring when the reserve is teeming with bird and insect life.

The route, which follows a traffic-free cyclepath most of the way, also crosses Easter Inch Moss, providing idyllic cycling in a quiet setting full of wildlife.

Further on, any young ones in your party will enjoy a visit to the farm at Almond Valley Heritage Centre, home to Highland cattle, rare breed sheep, goats, ponies, horses and some very inquisitive ducks. The centre also has a museum that graphically details Scotland's shale oil industry with an impressive array of artefacts.

Route 75 leads through Livingston to the Almondell and Calderwood Country Park, which is perhaps the highlight of the ride. Here you can enjoy the tranquil atmosphere of the park and even a barbecue.

The route then passes under the impressive Almondell Viaduct and alongside the River Almond before leading on to Kirknewton.

Almondell & Calderwood Country Park

ROUTE INFORMATION
National Route: 75
Start: Bathgate train station.
Finish: Kirknewton train station.
Distance: 12 miles (19.5km).
Grade: Easy.
Surface: Tarmac, with dust track in Almondell and Calderwood Country Park.
Hills: Small hills, but from the country park there is a long hill to Kirknewton.

YOUNG & INEXPERIENCED CYCLISTS
Traffic-free, apart from a section through Livingston village.

REFRESHMENTS
- Lots of choice in Bathgate and Livingston.
- Almondell and Calderwood Country Park Visitor Centre.
- Other options in East Calder and Kirknewton.

THINGS TO SEE & DO

- Bogburn Flood Lagoons, just off Route 75 near Bathgate: Scottish Wildlife Trust reserve consisting of three open freshwater pools surrounded by marshy grassland; 0131 312 7765; www.swt.org.uk
- Almond Valley Heritage Trust, Millfield, Livingston: working farm, watermill and museum nestled in a pleasant riverside site with woods and green spaces; 01506 414957; www.almondvalley.co.uk
- Almondell and Calderwood Country Park, Mid Calder: Route 75 passes through this 220-acre country park, which offers woodland and riverside walks, picnic areas and barbecue facilities (booking essential); 01506 882254; www.westlothian.gov.uk
- Malleny Garden, Balerno: 3-acre walled garden, renowned for its peaceful atmosphere, set in 9 acres of woodland and grounds; contains fine examples of ancient topiary and a collection of 19th-century shrub roses; 0844 493 2123; www.nts.org.uk

TRAIN STATIONS

Bathgate; Livingston North; Livingston South; Uphall; Kirknewton.

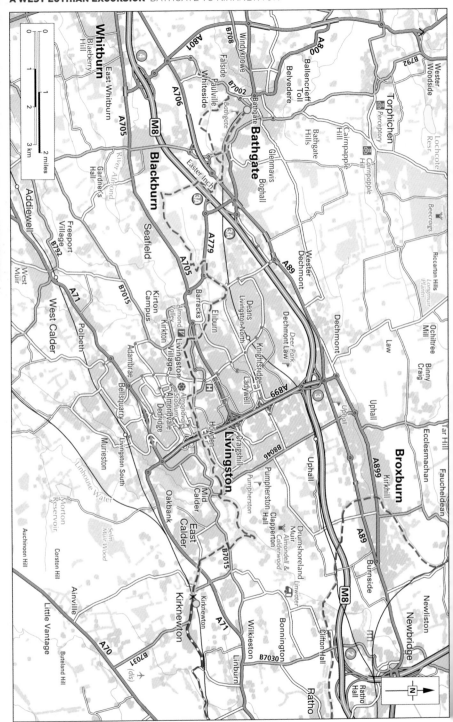

Malleny Garden, Balerno

BIKE HIRE

- Bathgate Bikes, Bathgate: 01506 632727
- Biketrax, Edinburgh: 0131 228 6633; www.biketrax.co.uk
- Cycle Scotland, Edinburgh: 0131 556 5560; www.cyclescotland.co.uk

FURTHER INFORMATION

- To view or print National Cycle Network routes, visit www.sustrans.org.uk
- Maps for this area are available to buy from www.sustransshop.co.uk
- For further information on routes in Scotland, visit www.routes2ride.org.uk/scotland
- Scotland Tourist Information: 0845 225 5121; 0131 625 8625; www.visitscotland.com

ROUTE DESCRIPTION

Turn left from Bathgate station and take the B7002 (Whitburn Road) south. Look out for signs to National Route 75 and follow it for 1.5 miles past the Bogburn Flood Lagoons Nature Reserve, then through a residential area to join the path near the supermarket. Alternatively, the most direct route to the path from Bathgate railway station is to turn right along King Street and continue on Edinburgh Road (A89) to Guildiehaugh roundabout. Turn right onto Blackburn Road and left onto the cyclepath just past the supermarket. This misses out the Bogburn Flood Lagoons. Follow the signs east to Edinburgh on the traffic-free cyclepath. This leads over the M8 and across Easter Inch Moss on a path to Livingston. Look for the Route 75 signs – there's a network of cyclepaths in the town. The route passes close to the Almond Valley Heritage Trust before entering old Livingston village. Further east the route runs parallel to the River Almond, to pass through Mid Calder. The cyclepath crosses the river then enters the Almondell and Calderwood Country Park. Route 75 now climbs from the river, crosses the B7015, and continues on a farm track almost directly opposite. Further on,

the route crosses a busy junction (dismount) and continues along a minor road that leads uphill to Kirknewton train station, which has a regular train service to Edinburgh.

NEARBY CYCLE ROUTES

The Bathgate to Kirknewton trail is part of the Clyde to Forth Route (National Route 75) which extends from Portavadie on the Cowal Peninsula to Glasgow and continues across Scotland to Edinburgh.

The Union Canal (National Route 754) passes near the route and can be accessed by following the signed link for 2 miles on minor roads from the Country Park visitor centre to the canal, via the curiously named Lookaboutye.

In Almondell and Calderwood Country Park, Route 75 goes under the towering Camp Viaduct near East Calder. When you reach the B7015, look for signs on the right which lead you over the viaduct and onto a pleasant path to Uphall station and to Uphall and Broxburn.

A number of commuter cyclepaths lead through Livingston.

There are excellent mountain bike trails in the Pentland Hills. Check suitability at www.edinburgh.gov.uk/phrp.

The Water of Leith path starts at Balerno.

UNION CANAL – LINLITHGOW TO THE FALKIRK WHEEL

Enjoy a fine cycle along one of the flattest routes in the country, running alongside the Union Canal. Being a contour canal, there are no locks and, instead, it follows the lie of the land, seeking the gentlest gradient possible.

The Union Canal was between 1817 and 1882, linking the city of Edinburgh with the Forth & Clyde Canal at Falkirk. In its heyday, there were a number of basins in the capital, where coal and building materials were offloaded for the fast-growing city, and hides were taken back to the tanneries in Linlithgow and Falkirk. Passengers travelled the route, too.

The construction of the canal was an engineering triumph, which necessitated the building of the Avon Aqueduct – the second longest aqueduct in the UK – and the 631m (2,070ft) long Falkirk Tunnel. The latter was hewn out of rock so that a local landowner wouldn't be disturbed by passing traffic!

The route leads on to an impressive view of the futuristic-looking Falkirk Wheel, which joins the Union and Forth & Clyde Canals together by way of its unique rotating boat lift.

Falkirk Wheel detail

ROUTE INFORMATION
National Route: 754
Start: Linlithgow train station.
Finish: Falkirk Wheel.
Distance: 11 miles (17.5km).
Grade: Easy.
Surface: Stone dust.
Hills: None.

YOUNG & INEXPERIENCED CYCLISTS
Ideal for novices and families with young children. A long tunnel section, directly east of Falkirk High train station, might prove intimidating but it can be bypassed on a ramp to the right (see 'Country Paths in and around The Falkirk Wheel and South Falkirk', free from Falkirk Council on 01324 506070).

REFRESHMENTS
- Lots of choice in Linlithgow.
- Linlithgow Canal Centre tearoom, Linlithgow.
- Falkirk Wheel Cafe, Falkirk Wheel Visitor Centre.

THINGS TO SEE & DO
- Linlithgow Palace, Linlithgow: roofless but still majestic 15th-century royal palace of the

The full splendour of the Falkirk Wheel

Stewarts; 01506 842896; www.historic-scotland.gov.uk

- **Linlithgow Canal Centre:** housed in a former canal stable, this museum details the history of the Union Canal; there is also information on local wildlife; 01506 671215; www.lucs.org.uk
- **The Falkirk Wheel:** innovative boat lift joining central Scotland's two canals by way of a rotating caisson; boat trips available as well as a good visitor centre; 0870 050 0208; www.thefalkirkwheel.co.uk

TRAIN STATIONS
Linlithgow; Polmont; Falkirk High.

BIKE HIRE
- **Leith Cycle Co, Leith:** 0131 467 7775; www.leithcycleco.com
- **Biketrax, Edinburgh:** 0131 228 6633; www.biketrax.co.uk
- **Cycle Scotland, Edinburgh:** 0131 556 5560; www.cyclescotland.co.uk

FURTHER INFORMATION
- To view or print National Cycle Network routes, visit www.sustrans.org.uk
- Maps for this area are available to buy from www.sustransshop.co.uk

- For further information on routes in Scotland, visit www.routes2ride.org.uk/scotland
- **West Lothian Tourist Information:** www.visitwestlothian.co.uk
- **Scotland Tourist Information:** 0845 225 5121; 0131 625 8625; www.visitscotland.com

Cycling along Union Canal, Edinburgh

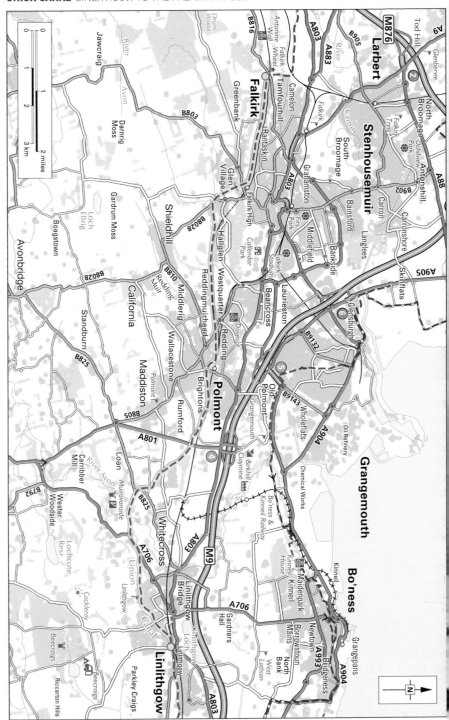

Canoeists on the
Avon Aqueduct

ROUTE DESCRIPTION

From the ticket office side (Edinburgh-bound) of Linlithgow train station, turn left, go under a tunnel, to reach the canal and turn right (the Linlithgow Canal Centre lies opposite); from the southern platform, follow the road uphill to meet the canal.

The towpath leads westwards and, after 3 miles (5km), crosses the Avon Aqueduct, where you will need to dismount to cross.

Continue to cycle by Polmont, with views towards the Ochil Hills, to reach the Falkirk Tunnel. This 631m (2,070ft) long tunnel passes under Prospect Hill and can be daunting as it is gloomily lit – bring a light. An alternative route can be accessed by a ramp before the tunnel mouth (see under 'Young & Inexperienced Cyclists'). The far end comes out close to Falkirk High train station.

Further on, a newly built section of the canal leads through Roughcastle Tunnel to emerge by the Falkirk Wheel. From there you could return 2 miles (3km) to Falkirk High station, which is signed from the canal towpath.

NEARBY CYCLE ROUTES

The Linlithgow to Falkirk Wheel trail is part of National Route 754, which links Edinburgh with Glasgow by following the Union and Forth & Clyde Canals.

The Round the Forth Route currently follows the coast from Berwick-upon-Tweed to Edinburgh, to Stirling and Kirkcaldy. In time, it is planned to extend the route round the East Neuk of Fife to St Andrews.

The Clyde to Forth Route (National Route 75), which connects Leith with Edinburgh and extends west to Glasgow, Gourock and the Cowal Peninsula, passes to the south of Linlithgow.

Just to the south of Falkirk, there is an interesting network of paths in Callander House Estate, which provide some nice circular cycling routes.

ROMAN ENCOUNTERS – GALASHIELS TO DRYBURGH

The Romans conquered many peoples but they never quite managed to get one over on the Pictish barbarians. It wasn't for lack of trying, though, as they set up a chain of outposts north of Hadrian's Wall. By AD 80, a road from Dover to Aberdeen linked a string of forts, and Trimontium near Melrose was the most important on the road between the Rivers Tyne and Forth.

This extensive fort can be easily visited from Melrose (by following the signed Four Abbeys Route) and is just one of the quality attractions along this route that has some very enjoyable traffic-free sections on closed roads.

Also in Melrose, Route 1 passes right by Melrose Abbey, founded in the early 12th century. Although a ruin, it is still a beautiful building with an air of grandeur about it. Robert the Bruce's heart is reputed to have been buried here.

The route continues, with views to the conical Eildon Hills, ending at Dryburgh Abbey, located at a pretty bend in the River Tweed.

ROUTE INFORMATION

National Route: 1
Start: Currie Road, Galashiels.
Finish: Dryburgh Abbey.
Distance: 8 miles (13km).
Grade: Easy.
Surface: Tarmac.
Hills: Mainly flat, but a steady climb after Melrose, into Eildon.

YOUNG & INEXPERIENCED CYCLISTS

This route is ideal for novices and young children, except for an on-road section through Melrose and Newtown St Boswells, and a subsequent crossing of the A68.

REFRESHMENTS

Lots of choice in Galashiels and Melrose.

THINGS TO SEE & DO

- **Melrose Town Trail:** self-led walking trail starting and finishing at the Tourist Information Centre in Abbey House, opposite Melrose Abbey. The trail is approximately 2.5 miles (4km) long and takes about two hours.
- **Trimontium Heritage Centre, Melrose:** the Roman era through aerial photographs, artists' drawings, models, replica armour and a video room; 01896 822651; www.trimontium.org.uk
- **Melrose Abbey:** magnificent 14th-century ruin on a grand scale, with lavishly decorated masonry; a small museum houses a display of artefacts found inside the abbey; 01896 822562; www.historic-scotland.gov.uk
- **Dryburgh Abbey**, on the B6404, near St Boswells: established in 1150, Dryburgh Abbey became the premier house in Scotland of the Premonstratensian order; set in a

Dryburgh Abbey

Melrose town centre

beautiful wooded location by the River Tweed; 01835 822381; www.historic-scotland.gov.uk

TRAIN STATIONS
None nearby.

BIKE HIRE
- Singletrack Bikes, Galashiels: 01896 758327; www.singletrackbikes.co.uk
- Diamond Cycle Centre, Galashiels: 01896 758410 www.stevediamondcycles.co.uk

Inscription to Robert the Bruce, Melrose Abbey

FURTHER INFORMATION
- To view or print National Cycle Network routes, visit www.sustrans.org.uk
- Maps for this area are available to buy from www.sustransshop.co.uk

- For further information on routes in Scotland, visit www.routes2ride.org.uk/scotland
- Melrose Tourist Information: 01835 822283; www.visitscottishborders.com
- Scotland Tourist Information: 0845 225 5121; 0131 625 8625; www.visitscotland.com

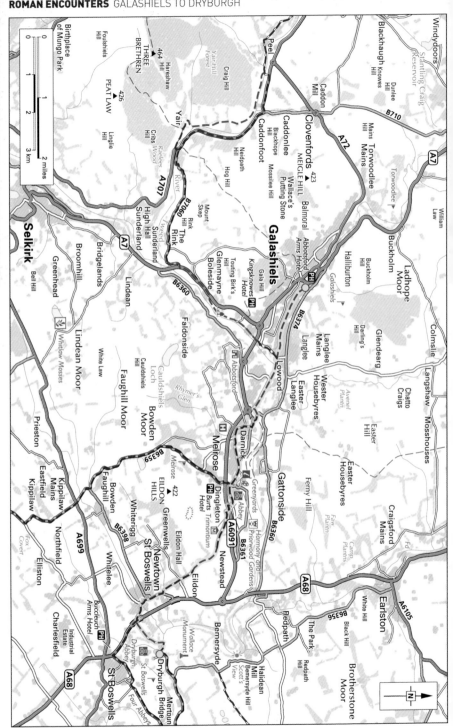

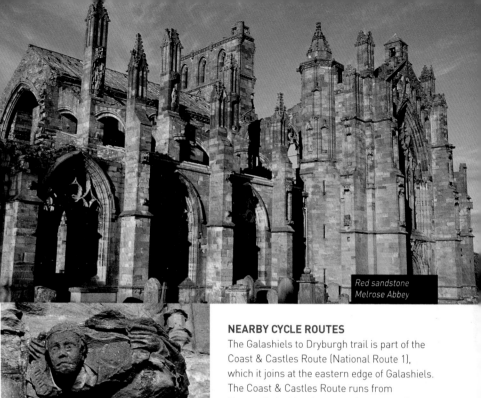

Red sandstone
Melrose Abbey

Carving on the side
of Melrose Abbey

ROUTE DESCRIPTION

From Currie Road in the centre of Galashiels, join the traffic-free cyclepath by the river. This follows a 3-mile (5km) path along a disused railway line to Darnick. Just before it crosses the River Tweed, it is joined by National Route 1, southbound for Melrose.

From Darnick, there is an on-road section that leads through Melrose. On the far side of Melrose, beyond Melrose Abbey, the route crosses the A6091, where a 2-mile (3km) section of closed road (no through traffic) leads to Newtown St Boswells.

An on-road section of Route 1 runs through the town and to a crossing of the busy A68 trunk road. On the far side, a no-through road takes cyclists down to a picturesque footbridge over the River Tweed and on to Dryburgh Abbey.

NEARBY CYCLE ROUTES

The Galashiels to Dryburgh trail is part of the Coast & Castles Route (National Route 1), which it joins at the eastern edge of Galashiels. The Coast & Castles Route runs from Newcastle to Aberdeen, passing areas of historic interest and pretty coastline.

South of Galashiels, on Route 1, there is a 2-mile (3km) section on a no-through road and cycle track along the River Tweed near Boleside. Another traffic-free section of Route 1 runs between Peel and Yair, which are linked by a 2-mile (3km) roughly surfaced farm track. Both rides are ideal for families.

The Four Abbeys Cycle Route is a 55-mile (88.5km) circular route that links the four main abbeys in the Scottish Borders: Melrose, Dryburgh, Kelso and Jedburgh. The route follows mainly quiet roads, although short stretches on 'A' roads are unavoidable.

The nearby 7stanes centres at Glentress and Innerleithen afford some of the best mountain biking in the UK. Innerleithen is for experts only, but Glentress has something for all levels, including a skills park (www.7stanes.gov.uk).

Sustrans and Scottish Borders Council are constructing a traffic-free route along the old railway line between Innerleithen and Peebles which should be complete by 2013.

STRATHCLYDE LOCH TO CHATELHERAULT COUNTRY PARK

This new walking and cycling route links Chatelherault and Strathclyde Country Parks and is part of a wider project to link the towns of Hamilton and Larkhall with a combination of traffic-free and traffic-calmed paths. This provides a safe haven for walkers and cyclists to enjoy the peace and wildlife away from the noisy M74.

Strathclyde Country Park, which is home to the Strathclyde Loch, is next to the River Clyde. When the loch was created in the early 1970s it involved flooding the old mining village of Bothwellhaugh. The remains of Bothwellhaugh Roman fort and a Roman bath house can be seen in the park, where the South Calder Water flows into the loch. There is an arched Roman bridge across the South Calder nearby. The site of the Battle of Bothwell Bridge (1679) is to the northwest. The loch has a famous sporting tradition as site of the Commonwealth Games rowing events in 1986, and the 2014 Commonwealth Games triathlon. Chatelherault Country Park is a beautiful area with walks along the Avon Water against picturesque woodland. The bulk of the park lies along the Avon Gorge.

ROUTE INFORMATION

Start: Strathclyde Country Park.
Finish: Chatelherault Country Park.
Distance: 7 miles (11km).
Grade: Easy.
Surface: Tarmac and well-surfaced paths.
Hills: Gentle gradients along wide paths.

YOUNG & INEXPERIENCED CYCLISTS

The path is ideal for young and inexperienced cyclists and travels under and over a variety of bridges, successfully avoiding all the busy roads into Hamilton.

REFRESHMENTS

- Watersports centre and cafe at Strathclyde Country Park.
- Chatelherault Country Park cafe.

THINGS TO SEE & DO

- Strathclyde Country Park Watersports Centre: rowing, windsurfing, dinghy sailing, canoeing, water skiing, pedalos, bumper boats, boat trips, wavebobs and Canadian canoes. Craft are available for hire; 01698 402060; www.visitlanarkshire.com
- Chatelherault Country Park: over 10 miles (16km) of stunning gorge walks along the Avon Water and through ancient woodland, some of which is the oldest in the country. The area is home to a wide range of wildlife including roe deer, badgers, otters, kingfishers and more. Visitors to the lodge can also view the Duke's private Banqueting Room, apartments and formal gardens; 01698 426213; www.visitlanarkshire.com

TRAIN STATIONS

Chatelherault; Hamilton Central; Airbles.

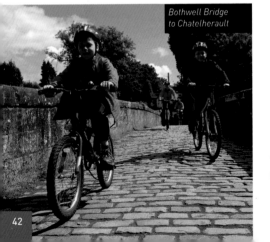

Bothwell Bridge to Chatelherault

Strathclyde Country Park at dawn

BIKE HIRE
None locally.

FURTHER INFORMATION
- To view or print National Cycle Network routes, visit www.sustrans.org.uk
- Lanarkshire Tourist Information: www.visitlanarkshire.com

ROUTE DESCRIPTION
The route starts at the north end of Strathclyde Loch. There is a traffic-free tarmac path along the majority of the west bank of the loch, so keeping the loch to your left and the River Clyde to your right, head south towards the watersports centre. On joining the quiet road, turn right for the exit to the country park just after the car park and before you reach the watersports centre pier. Cross the road and the cycling and walking bridge over the River Clyde. Turn left just before the underbridge beneath the M74 and follow the route round, slowing up for the pinch point under the A723 red Clyde Bridge. Continue on the traffic-free path, which then follows the banks of the Avon Water to Haughhead, crossing the Covan Burn. Turn left to cross the river via the Old Avon Bridge and the route soon skirts the edge of Chatelherault Country Park as it takes you right in front of the main hunting lodge. From here you can access many of the trails around the park, including the West Glen Route, an established walking and cycling route through the leafy Avon Glen.

There are two further sections to the route in development. From Strathclyde Country Park, a further extension to the route continues straight on under the M74 underbridge, taking you past the Mausoleum and the wonderful Hamilton Racecourse. A new crossing at Caird Street and a wide footway along the full length of Bothwell Road have been improved, enabling pedestrians and cyclists to cross the busy road and travel to the outskirts of Hamilton.

Farther south at Chatelherault, further work is proposed to create a safe route for cyclists along Carlisle Road and down into Larkhall, a small town on the edge of the Avon Water.

STRATHCLYDE LOCH TO CHATELHERAULT COUNTRY PARK

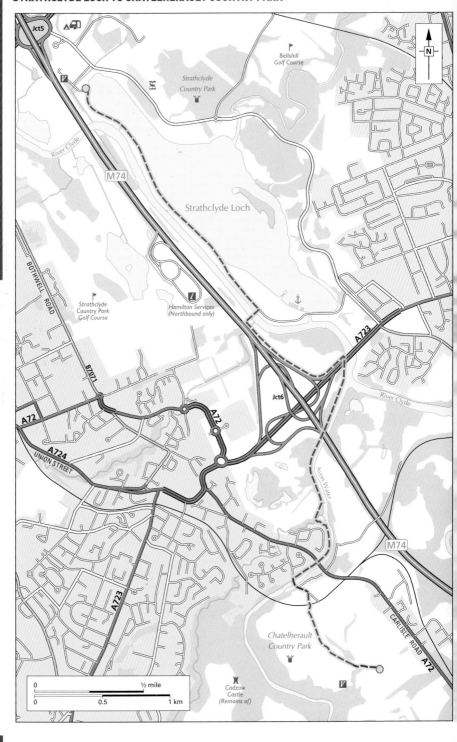

East wing of Chatelherault House

NEARBY CYCLE ROUTES

There are a number of trails at Chatelherault Country Park, including along the Avon Water.

On the east side of Strathclyde Loch the Greenlink route will take you on a very pleasant ride from the site of the Roman bath house past Bellshill Golf Club and on into the centre of Motherwell.

You can also cycle right around Strathclyde Loch. The route along its southern section is shared with the quiet road that services the watersports centre.

PAISLEY & CLYDE RAILWAY PATH – PAISLEY TO GOUROCK

This cyclepath makes a great day out from the city. It's easy to follow and provides ever more dramatic views as it progresses, from Paisley to Gourock, down the Firth of Clyde.

The route follows one branch of the long-defunct Glasgow & South-Western Railway (G&SWR), which passes the town of Johnstone and crosses attractive open country between Bridge of Weir and Kilmacolm, before reaching Port Glasgow, Greenock and Gourock. In 1850, the G&SWR became the third largest railway company in Scotland, formed by an amalgamation of smaller railways. More than half of its fleet were coal wagons. Other traffic hauled included fish from the Ayrshire ports, and machinery from works in the Glasgow and Renfrewshire areas.

As you leave Paisley, the route is full of the strong, musky scent of foxes. In Elderslie there is a short on-road section and the opportunity to visit the William Wallace Memorial. Pedal on, following Route 75, to cross an old viaduct before Bridge of Weir. This can be a good place for a break – the welcoming Gryffe Inn does no-frills bar meals and is worth a peek for the fine old photograph collection of the long-gone railway and chortling washerwomen.

On the outskirts of Port Glasgow the descent begins towards the Clyde and Gourock, where ferries cross to Dunoon, a gateway to the Cowal Peninsula area of the Loch Lomond and the Trossachs National Park.

'Sleeper Awake' artwork

Surface: Tarmac.
Hills: Steady but easy incline from Linwood to Port Glasgow, followed by two steep descents and a steep climb from Devol Glen.

YOUNG & INEXPERIENCED CYCLISTS

Because of the hills, the best section is from Paisley to Kilmacolm. Care needs to be taken at on-road sections. The signed route is 90 per cent traffic-free, apart from short sections through Elderslie and Kilmacolm and longer sections in Port Glasgow and Greenock.

ROUTE INFORMATION
National Routes: 7, 75
Start: Paisley Canal train station.
Finish: Gourock ferry terminal.
Distance: 23 miles (37km).
Grade: Moderate.

REFRESHMENTS
- Lots of choice in Paisley and in towns along the route.
- Gryffe Inn, Bridge of Weir.
- Pub on track on approach to Kilmacolm.

THINGS TO SEE & DO

- **Paisley Museum & Art Gallery:** lots of old artefacts and everyday items from the 1900s; 0141 889 3151; www.renfrewshire.gov.uk
- **William Wallace Memorial, Elderslie:** Elderslie, about 2 miles (3km) west of Paisley, is traditionally thought to be the birthplace of Scotland's Braveheart; www.renfrewshire.gov.uk
- **Newark Castle, Port Glasgow:** finely restored Jacobean castle with excellent views over the Firth of Clyde; 01475 741858; www.historic-scotland.gov.uk
- **Clyde Muirshiel Regional Park, south Clyde Estuary:** more than 100 square miles (160sq km) of moorland and upland grassland, with a sprinkling of reservoirs and lochs; an attractive place for cyclists and wildlife enthusiasts; 01475 521458 (Cornalees Visitor Centre); www.clydemuirshiel.co.uk

TRAIN STATIONS

Paisley Canal; Johnstone; Port Glasgow; Greenock Central; Gourock; plus intermediate stations.

BIKE HIRE

- Billy Bilsland Cycles, Saltmarket, Glasgow: 0141 552 0841; www.billybilslandcycles.co.uk
- Gear of Glasgow, Hillhead, Glasgow: 0141 339 1179; www.gearbikes.co.uk
- Castle Semple Visitor Centre, near Lochwinnoch: 01505 842882; www.clydemuirshiel.co.uk

FURTHER INFORMATION

- To view or print National Cycle Network routes, visit www.sustrans.org.uk
- Maps for this area are available to buy from www.sustransshop.co.uk
- For further information on routes in Scotland, visit: www.routes2ride.org.uk/scotland
- Paisley Tourist Information: 0141 889 0711

- Scotland Tourist Information: 0845 225 5121; 0131 625 8625; www.visitscotland.com

ROUTE DESCRIPTION

From Paisley Canal train station, follow the cyclepath to Elderslie where, after a short on-road section, signs for Route 7 and 75 lead right. Further on, at a multicoloured steel sculpture, turn right to follow Route 75 (Route 7 goes left).

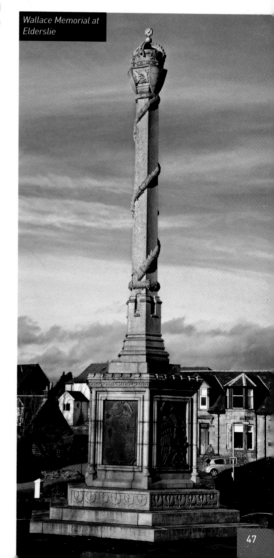

Wallace Memorial at Elderslie

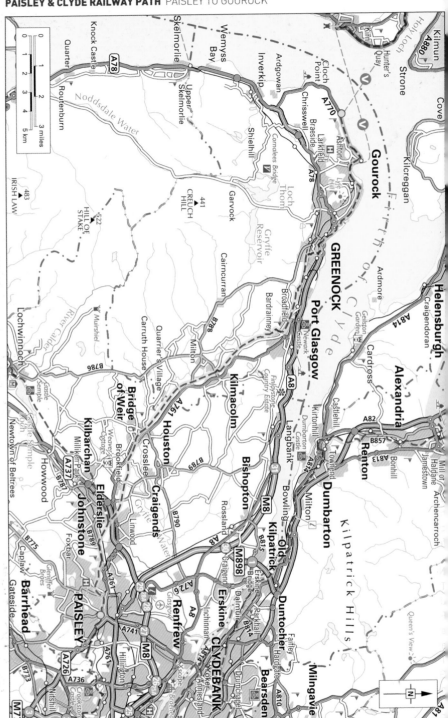

Newark Castle and
Ferguson's shipyard

After Kilmacolm, descend to Port Glasgow and follow signs for the on-road sections here and later into Greenock. From there, the route hugs the coast on a largely traffic-free cyclepath to finish the ride at the Gourock ferry terminal.

NEARBY CYCLE ROUTES

The Paisley & Clyde Railway Path is part of the longer Clyde to Forth Route (National Route 75), which connects Leith with Edinburgh and extends west to Glasgow and Gourock, and across the Cowal Peninsula to Portavadie. To the east, it passes through the centre of Glasgow and continues to Edinburgh via the new Airdrie to Bathgate Railway Path.

The section of the Paisley & Clyde Railway Path from Paisley to just beyond Johnstone is shared with the Lochs & Glens Route (National Route 7), which runs from Carlisle to Inverness.

North of Kilmacolm, an off-road route allows adventurous cyclists to ride by Loch Thom in the Clyde Muirshiel Regional Park and into Greenock. The middle section of the route is best suited to mountain bikes.

The Lochwinnoch Loop Line is a family-friendly 14-mile (22.5km) cycle ride that follows Route 75 from Paisley Canal station to Johnstone. It then heads southwest to Kilbarchan, Lochwinnoch and Kilbirnie, passing Castle Semple, Barr and Kilbirnie Lochs (see page 58). Most of the route is traffic-free. If you wish, you can do the return journey by train from Lochwinnoch station.

BOWLING TO THE FALKIRK WHEEL

Scotland's principal cities, Glasgow and Edinburgh, are linked by two canals: the Forth & Clyde Canal from Bowling to Falkirk and the Union Canal from Falkirk to Edinburgh. Together they offer a wonderful, level cycling route through Scotland's central belt, with the Falkirk Wheel representing the highlight of the whole route at the junction of the two canals. The ride described here follows the section along the Forth & Clyde from Bowling, near Glasgow, to the Falkirk Wheel.

The Forth & Clyde Canal opened in 1790 and the Union Canal opened in 1822. They fell into disuse in the early 1960s, but then, as part of the Millennium celebrations in 2000, the £78 million Millennium Link project was set in motion to restore navigability across Scotland on the Forth & Clyde and Union Canals.

A major challenge was to create a link between the two canals at Falkirk, as the Forth & Clyde Canal lay well below the level of the Union Canal. Historically, the two canals had been joined by a flight of locks, but these were dismantled in 1933. The answer was the perfectly balanced structure known as the Falkirk Wheel – the world's first and only rotating boat lift – opened by the Queen in 2002. The Wheel is the height of eight double-decker buses and is capable of lifting loads equivalent to the weight of 100 elephants!

ROUTE INFORMATION
National Routes: 754, 7
Start: Bowling Harbour on the Clyde Estuary, west of Glasgow.
Finish: Falkirk Wheel.
Distance: 30 miles (48km).
Grade: Easy to moderate.
Surface: Gravel and tarmac.
Hills: None.

YOUNG & INEXPERIENCED CYCLISTS
Traffic-free, except for Stockingfield Junction, Glasgow, which involves negotiating the road for a short stretch.

REFRESHMENTS
- Lots of choice in Clydebank, Glasgow and Kirkintilloch.
- See www.scottishcanals.co.uk for details of eating places along the Forth & Clyde Canal.
- Boathouse pub, Auchinstarry Marina.
- Cafe at the Falkirk Wheel.

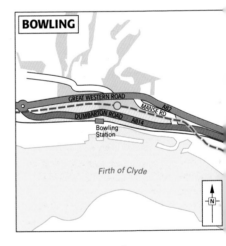

THINGS TO SEE & DO
- **Clydebank Museum:** local, social and industrial history artefacts, especially relating to ship-building; 0141 562 2400; www.museumsgalleriesscotland.org.uk
- **Auld Kirk Museum, Kirkintilloch:** local history collection housed in a building dating from 1644; 0141 578 0144;

Boats in the Forth
& Clyde Canal

www.museumsgalleriesscotland.org.uk
- **Antonine Wall**: name given to the Roman frontier in Scotland, which crossed the narrowest part of Britain, from Bo'ness, on the Firth of Forth, to Old Kilpatrick, on the River Clyde; passes very close to the Falkirk Wheel; www.antonine-way.co.uk
- **Rough Castle Roman Fort**: small but well-preserved fort on the Antonine Wall; can be reached by footpaths from the Falkirk Wheel; www.antonine-way.co.uk
- **Falkirk Wheel**: boat trips, cafe, picnic area and interactive exhibition; 0870 050 0208; www.thefalkirkwheel.co.uk
- **Falkirk Museums**: collections local to the Falkirk area, including Roman archaeology relating to the Antonine Wall, iron-founding artefacts and items from the potteries in Bo'ness and Dunmore; 01324 503770; www.museumsgalleriesscotland.org.uk

The Falkirk
Wheel aqueduct

TRAIN STATIONS
Bowling and all stations into the centre of Glasgow; Croy; Camelon; Falkirk Grahamston; Falkirk High (access to the canal from the south station platform).

BIKE HIRE
- Magic Cycles, Bowling Harbour: 01389 873433; www.magiccycles.co.uk
- Billy Bilsland Cycles, Saltmarket, Glasgow: 0141 552 0841; www.billybilslandcycles.co.uk

FURTHER INFORMATION
- To view or print National Cycle Network routes, visit www.sustrans.org.uk
- Maps for this area are available to buy from www.sustransshop.co.uk
- For more information on routes in Scotland, visit www.routes2ride.org.uk/scotland
- Glasgow Tourist Information: www.seeglasgow.com
- Scotland Tourist Information: 0845 225 5121; www.visitscotland.com

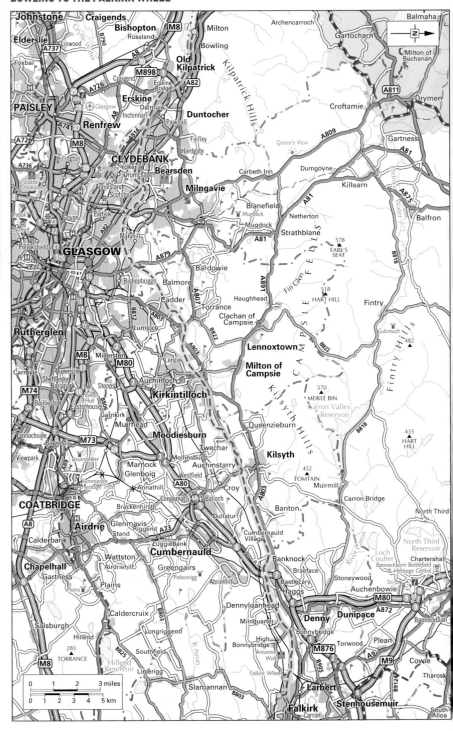

The awesome Falkirk Wheel

ROUTE DESCRIPTION

The ride is usually best done from west to east, as this is the direction of the prevailing wind. Start on National Route 7 at Bowling, where the Forth & Clyde Canal enters the Clyde. Pass through Clydebank, where Route 7 heads off alongside the River Clyde towards the centre of Glasgow, and Route 754 continues on the canal, passing the imposing Maryhill Locks.

Alternatively, if starting from central Glasgow, you can take the Kelvin Walkway to the locks at Maryhill or follow the branch canal north from Port Dundas for 2 miles (3km) until it meets the main canal at the Stockingfield Junction. Along this elevated section, there are fine views right across the city. Take care making the connection at Stockingfield, as you have to leave the canal for a short section on a difficult road – a bridge is planned to solve the problem here.

After Stockingfield, you reach Glasgow Road Bridge, a bustling boating, eating and drinking centre. From here, you shortly come to the beautiful Kelvin Valley, with the Kilsyth Hills to the north. Follow the canal through Kirkintilloch, the Auchinstarry Marina and on to Bonnybridge, from where it's only another

3 miles (5km) to the Falkirk Wheel. From here, you can follow the path up beside the wheel until you pass through a short tunnel onto the Union Canal towards Linlithgow and eventually Edinburgh (the full distance from Bowling to Edinburgh is 62 miles/100km). Once you get onto the canal, it's hard to get lost!

To return, you can access the south platform of Falkirk High train station from the canal for trains back to either Glasgow or Edinburgh.

NEARBY CYCLE ROUTES

National Route 7 heads north from Bowling to Loch Lomond, Pitlochry and Inverness (see page 54). In the other direction, it follows the canal to Clydebank and then carries on parallel to the Clyde to Bell's Bridge in the centre of Glasgow, before heading down to Ayr and Carlisle. National Route 75 intersects with Route 7 at Bell's Bridge – it runs between Gourock on the Clyde and Leith (Edinburgh) on the Forth.

Other waymarked or traffic-free rides include the Kelvin Walkway, also a cycle route, which runs alongside the River Kelvin from Kelvinside to Milngavie. The Strathkelvin Railway Path runs from south of Muirhead, through Kirkintilloch to Strathblane.

CLYDE & LOCH LOMOND CYCLEWAY – BOWLING TO BALLOCH

For those who love easy-going cycling, this is the route for you. And, in addition to being a good and level ride, there's a dramatic finish by the shores of Loch Lomond to boot.

Following an old railway line between Bowling and Dumbarton, and then a riverside cyclepath onwards to Balloch, this is a route where navigation is very straightforward.

Before you start, you should take a small diversion down to Bowling Harbour. Here you can watch as the western end of the Forth & Clyde Canal spills into the River Clyde; there are good views down the widening firth, too.

A short on-road section leads through the town of Dumbarton, where you should make a second detour to visit the ancient Dumbarton Castle. Strategically positioned atop a high volcanic plug, it has a commanding view of the river. The castle last saw action during World War II, when it was used as a garrison fortress. In more recent years a daring raid was launched on the rock, when Scottish climber Dave MacLeod completed the hardest climb in the world on its sheer walls.

Continue through the Vale of Leven, where textile mills boomed during the Industrial Revolution. From there, Balloch is easily reached and you can enjoy superb views from the bonnie banks of Loch Lomond.

ROUTE INFORMATION
National Route: 7
Start: Bowling train station.
Finish: Balloch train station.
Distance: 9 miles (14.5km).

Grade: Easy.
Surface: Tarmac.
Hills: None.

YOUNG & INEXPERIENCED CYCLISTS
The whole route is traffic-free apart from a very short section through Dumbarton.

REFRESHMENTS
- Lots of choice, as the route passes close to many towns.

THINGS TO SEE & DO
- **Dumbarton Castle:** impressively situated on a volcanic rock, this fortress was the centre of the ancient kingdom of Strathclyde from the 5th century until 1018; more recently, it served as a garrison; 01389 732167; www.historic-scotland.gov.uk
- **Smollett Monument, Renton:** monument to Tobias Smollett, near his birthplace, commemorating this 18th-century novelist.
- **Loch Lomond and The Trossachs National Park Visitor Centre, Loch Lomond Shores,**

Drumkinnon Tower

Dumbarton Rock in the town of Dumbarton

Balloch: well-stocked visitor centre with a good display on the park's important natural history and geology; 01389 722600; www.lochlomond-trossachs.org
- Balloch Castle Country Park: popular attraction set within 200 acres of scenic country park; a network of paths crosses the park, which offer some very good views of Loch Lomond; 01389 722199; www.lochlomond-trossachs.org

TRAIN STATIONS

Bowling; Dumbarton East; Dumbarton Central; Dalreoch; Renton; Alexandria; Balloch.

BIKE HIRE

- Can You Experience, Balloch: 01389 756251; www.canyouexperience.com
- Magic Cycles, Bowling Harbour, 01389 873433; www.magiccycles.co.uk

FURTHER INFORMATION

- To view or print National Cycle Network routes, visit www.sustrans.org.uk
- Maps for this area are available to buy from www.sustransshop.co.uk
- For further information on routes in Scotland, visit www.routes2ride.org.uk/scotland
- Loch Lomond and The Trossachs National Park: 01389 722600; www.lochlomond-trossachs.org
- Scotland Tourist Information: 0845 225 5121;

CLYDE & LOCH LOMOND CYCLEWAY BOWLING TO BALLOCH

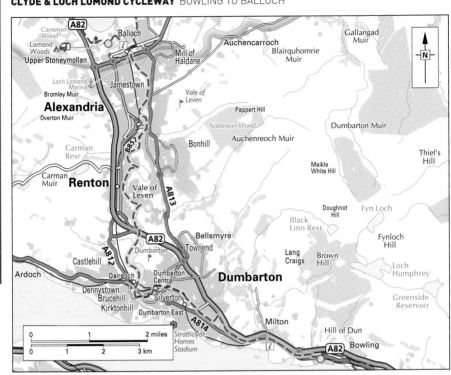

Loch Lomond near Balloch

0131 625 8625; www.visitscotland.com
• **Loch Lomond 4Bs (Boats, Boots, Bike and Bus):** information on cycling and walking routes around Loch Lomond, plus bike-bus and boat timetables; 0845 458 0885; www.lochlomond4bs.co.uk

ROUTE DESCRIPTION
The route is well signed throughout and easy to follow. From Bowling station, follow National Route 7 signs (for Dumbarton and Balloch) along a cyclepath with lovely views of the Firth of Clyde. Continue following the signs through Dumbarton to the southern end of the Vale of Leven. The cyclepath leads pleasantly alongside the River Leven to bring you directly to Balloch train station. From there it's worth continuing to Loch Lomond: turn right and then turn left through a car park and into a park where a cyclepath leads you to the National Park Gateway Centre and views up the length of Loch Lomond.

NEARBY CYCLE ROUTES
The Clyde & Loch Lomond Cycleway is part of the Lochs & Glens Route (National Route 7) – an interesting and varied route that runs from Sunderland to Carlisle and Inverness.

National Route 754 starts at Bowling, the western end of the Forth & Clyde Canal. This extends east to the Falkirk Wheel, where cyclists can join the Union Canal to continue to Edinburgh (see page 50). Sustrans is working with British Waterways to improve the towpath surfaces and remove barriers.

The West Loch Lomond Cyclepath (Regional Route 40) runs from Balloch to Tarbet. This dedicated cyclepath follows some very scenic sections to the north of Luss, where it runs right by the deep waters of Loch Lomond.

LOCHWINNOCH LOOPLINE – PAISLEY TO GLENGARNOCK

This route uses two dismantled railways running west from Johnstone: one heads northwest to Port Glasgow, then parallel with the coast to Greenock and Gourock; the other, the Lochwinnoch Loop Line, takes a more southerly direction, passing Castle Semple Loch, Barr Loch and Kilbirnie Loch.

The colour-washed houses in Lochwinnoch date from the early 19th century, when the village was a centre for cask- and barrel-making. The trail is part of the Lochs & Glens Cycle Route (National Route 7), which runs from Glasgow to Carlisle. There are long-term plans to extend the traffic-free section along the River Garnock Valley, from Kilbirnie to Kilwinning, thus bringing the dream of creating a traffic-free path all the way from Glasgow to the Ayrshire Coast one step closer.

Castle Semple Loch is a nationally recognized site for wild birds and a Site of Special Scientific Interest (SSSI). The visitor centre is an excellent location for water sports, walks, cycling and picnics. Boats and mountain bikes are available for hire. Near Kilbirnie, the route passes close to Glengarnock station, giving the option of taking the train for one leg of the trip to make best use of the prevailing wind.

ROUTE INFORMATION

National Routes: 7, 75
Start: Paisley Canal train station, southwest of Glasgow.
Finish: End of the railway path in Glengarnock.
Distance: 14 miles (22.5km).
Grade: Easy.
Surface: Tarmac.
Hills: There is a gentle climb south from Lochwinnoch to a highpoint about halfway towards Kilbirnie.

YOUNG & INEXPERIENCED CYCLISTS

There is one short section through Elderslie where care should be taken on the busy B789 (you may prefer to walk along the pavement). You will need to use short stretches of road if you visit Kilbirnie for refreshments.

REFRESHMENTS

- Garthland Arms pub, Brown Bull pub and Junction Cafe in Lochwinnoch.
- Basic cafe, fish and chip shop and Bowery pub in Kilbirnie.

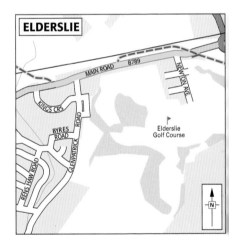

THINGS TO SEE & DO

- **Paisley Abbey:** dating from 1163; www.paisleyabbey.org.uk
- **Paisley Museum and Art Galleries:** 19th-century museum and art gallery housing a world-famous collection of Paisley shawls; 0141 889 3151; www.museumsgalleriesscotland.org.uk
- **Sma' Shot Cottages, Kilbarchan:** 18th-century weaver's cottage with exhibition

Boats on Castle Semple Loch

room, weaver's living area and loom room, all furnished in period style; 0141 889 1708; www.smashot.co.uk

- **Castle Semple Country Park, Loch and Visitor Centre:** part of the Clyde Muirshiel Regional Park, an excellent location for water sports, walks, cycling and picnics. The Loch is a nationally recognized site for wild birds and a Site of Special Scientific Interest (SSSI). Boats and mountain bikes are available for hire; 01505 842882; www.clydemuirshiel.co.uk

'The Ring' by David Annand, Kilwinning

- **Castle Semple Collegiate Church:** late Gothic church located next to Castle Semple and Barr Lochs; www.historic-scotland.gov.uk
- **Lochwinnoch Nature Reserve:** one of the few wetlands in west Scotland, with swans, geese, ducks and great crested grebes; 01505 842663; www.rspb.org.uk

TRAIN STATIONS

Paisley Canal; Johnstone; Howwood; Lochwinnoch; Glengarnock; and many more.

BIKE HIRE

- **Castle Semple Visitor Centre:** 01505 842882; www.clydemuirshiel.co.uk
- **RT Cycles and Fishing, Glengarnock:** 01505 682191; www.cyclerepairman.co.uk

FURTHER INFORMATION

- To view or print National Cycle Network routes, visit www.sustrans.org.uk
- Maps for this area are available to buy from www.sustransshop.co.uk
- For more information on routes in Scotland, visit www.routes2ride.org.uk/scotland
- **Paisley Tourist Information:** 0141 889 0711
- **Scotland Tourist Information:** 0845 225 5121; 0131 625 8625; www.visitscotland.com

ROUTE DESCRIPTION

After a safe, traffic-free section running west from Paisley Canal train station, there is a short stretch through Elderslie on the B789. A one-way system operates on the cycle route through Elderslie – follow the signs for National Route 7. You soon rejoin the course of the old

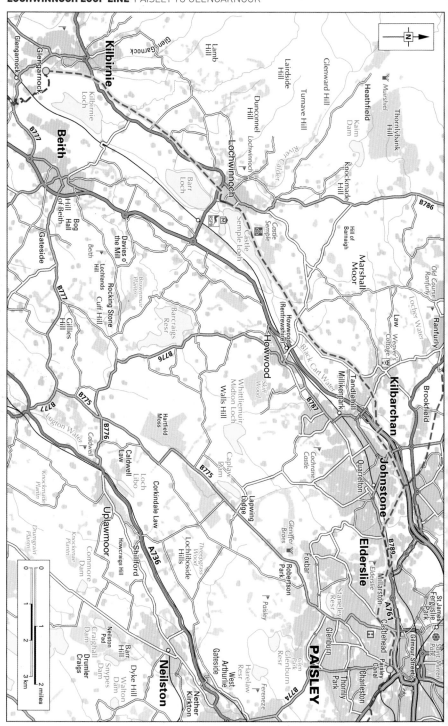

Blue tit at RSPB Lochwinnoch

'Sentinel' by Jim Paulsen

Footbridge over the River Garnock

railway, passing the dramatic *Aurora Borealis* sculpture at the junction of Routes 7 and 75. There are historic attractions along the way, including Lochwinnoch Temple and Castle Semple Collegiate Church.

The railway path continues along the glittering expanse of Castle Semple Loch and Barr Loch, passing the villages of Lochwinnoch and Kilbirnie, and finishes on the edge of Glengarnock.

A short detour on a cycle track from Route 7 in Lochwinnoch (head towards the train station) takes you to the RSPB visitor centre, where there are viewing hides. The best, most easily accessed refreshments are either in the village of Lochwinnoch or in Castle Semple Country Park Visitor Centre.

You can catch the train back at several points along the route – Kilbirnie is served by Glengarnock station.

NEARBY CYCLE ROUTES

National Route 7 (the Lochs & Glens Cycle Route) continues southwest beyond Kilbirnie to the Ayrshire Coast. To the north, beyond Paisley, Route 7 continues into the centre of Glasgow, crosses Bell's Bridge and then follows the Firth of Clyde and the River Leven to Loch Lomond on its way to the Highlands.

National Route 75 (the Clyde to Forth Cycle Route) goes west from Paisley to Johnstone, then continues south of the Firth of Clyde to Greenock and Gourock (see page 46). To the east, it passes through the centre of Glasgow and continues to Edinburgh via the new Airdrie to Bathgate Railway Path.

Other waymarked or traffic-free rides include:
- The Forth & Clyde Canal towpath.
- The Clyde & Loch Lomond Cycleway through Dumbarton to Loch Lomond.
- The Paisley & Clyde Railway Path.
- The Clyde Corridor Cycle Route east of Glasgow Green.

VARIED LANDSCAPES – AYR TO ARDROSSAN

This 28-mile (45km) route takes in long stretches of the Ayrshire coastline between Irvine, Troon, Prestwick and Ayr, and has spectacular views across to the Isle of Arran. Passing through three nature reserves at Stevenston Beach, Garnock Floods and Shewalton Moss, it offers the opportunity to experience the varied landscapes of this part of Scotland. You can visit glorious beaches or stop and explore the town centres along the way. It is also possible to organize shorter cycling trips by using the regular train service between Kilwinning and Ayr.

Ayr is the region's main coastal resort, dominated by the early 19th-century Town Buildings with their octagonal turret and 38m (125ft) steeple. Two bridges span the River Ayr: the Auld Brig dates from the 13th century and the New Bridge from 1788. Troon is famous for its golf courses (there are no fewer than five of them!) and its Victorian turreted red-sandstone buildings looking out over the sandy beach, marina and harbour to Ayr Bay. Ardrossan is the port serving the Isle of Arran, whose outline is a constant companion along the route.

ROUTE INFORMATION
National Routes: 7, 73
Start: Southern end of Ayr Esplanade.
Finish: Ardrossan ferry terminal.
Distance: 28 miles (45km). Shorter options: from Ayr to Irvine 19 miles (30.5km); from Irvine to Ardrossan 9 miles (14.5km).
Grade: Easy.
Surface: Tarmac.
Hills: None.

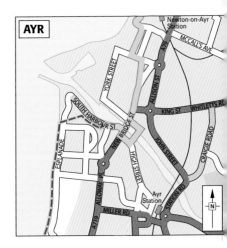

YOUNG & INEXPERIENCED CYCLISTS
Almost traffic-free with short on-road sections in Ayr, Prestwick, Troon and Irvine, and through residential streets in Barassie. About 2 miles (3km) on quiet roads between Kilwinning and Stevenston.

REFRESHMENTS
- Lots of choice in Ayr, Troon and Gailes.
- Cafe at the Maritime Museum, Irvine.
- The Ship Inn, Irvine.

THINGS TO SEE & DO
- Burns Birthplace Museum, Alloway, just south of Ayr: museum dedicated to Robert Burns; 01292 443700; www.burnsheritagepark.com

- Golf courses at Troon: includes Royal Troon Golf Club, host to the Open Golf Championship; 01292 311555 www.royaltroon.co.uk
- Dundonald Castle: dating back to the 1370s; 01563 851489; www.dundonaldcastle.org.uk
- Irvine Beach Park: includes a lake and leisure centre; www.ayrshirescotland.com
- Gailes Marsh Wildlife Reserve, Shewalton Wood Wildlife Reserve and Garnock Floods

Legendary Brig o' Doon in Alloway

Nature Reserve: good birdwatching sites;
www.swt.org.uk
- **Scottish Maritime Museum, Irvine:** a range
  of exhibits relating to Scotland's maritime
  history, including the Linthouse engine shop,
  a Victorian glass-roofed building dating from
  1872; 01294 278283;
  www.scottishmaritimemuseum.org;
  www.museumsgalleriesscotland.org.uk
- **Eglinton Country Park:** developed around the
  ancient Eglinton Estate, with a visitor centre,
  cafe and children's play area; 01294 551776;
  www.north-ayrshire.gov.uk

TRAIN STATIONS
Ayr; Newton-on-Ayr; Prestwick Town;
Prestwick International Airport; Troon;
Barassie; Irvine; Kilwinning; Stevenston;
Saltcoats; Ardrossan.

FERRIES
Ardrossan to Brodick ferry: www.calmac.co.uk

BIKE HIRE
- **RT Cycles and Fishing, Glengarnock:** delivers
  and collects cycles; 01505 682191;
  www.cyclerepairman.co.uk

FURTHER INFORMATION
- To view or print National Cycle Network
  routes, visit www.sustrans.org.uk
- Maps for this area are available to buy from
  www.sustransshop.co.uk
- For more information on routes in Scotland,
  visit www.routes2ride.org.uk/scotland
- **Ayrshire Tourist Information:**
  www.ayrshire-arran.com
- **Scotland Tourist Information:** 0845 225 5121;
  0131 625 8625; www.visitscotland.com

ROUTE DESCRIPTION
Between Ayr and Troon, the route is either on
or close to the coast. From Troon, it heads
inland and through two Scottish Wildlife Trust
reserves, Shewalton Wood and Gailes Marsh, to
return to the coast at Irvine Beach Park. It then
follows the riverside path through Irvine
towards Kilwinning, passing the Garnock
Floods Nature Reserve. Eglinton Country Park
is just off the route and offers extensive
opportunities for walking, cycling, horse-riding
and angling, plus children's play areas.

At Kilwinning, the route turns west along
minor roads to Stevenston, before rejoining a
traffic-free path, which runs along the coast

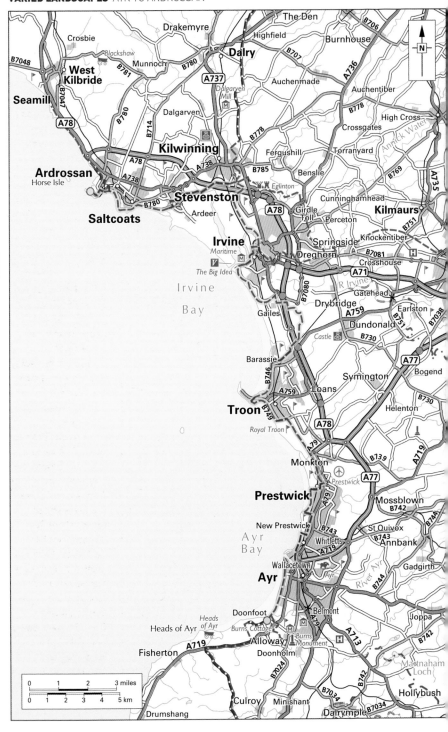

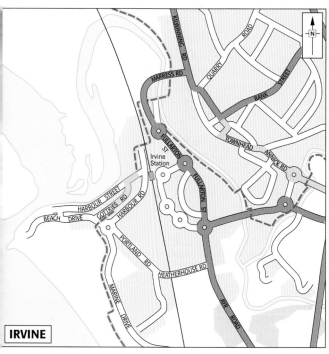

IRVINE

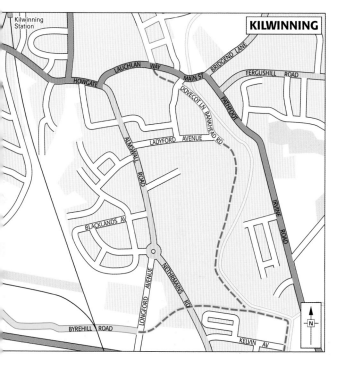

KILWINNING

and gives sweeping views towards the Isle of Arran. At Ardrossan, you can take your bike on the ferry to the Isle of Arran, known as 'Scotland in miniature', where the route continues from Brodick to Lochranza, or you can catch the train back to Irvine or Ayr.

NEARBY CYCLE ROUTES

National Route 7 heads north from Kilwinning to Lochwinnoch, Paisley and Glasgow. From Ayr, Route 7 continues to Newton Stewart, Dumfries and Carlisle. National Route 73 runs from Irvine to Kilmarnock. The ferry from Ardrossan will take you to the Isle of Arran, where Route 73 heads north to Lochranza. Here, another ferry links to National Route 78, running from Campbeltown to Oban. The New Town Trail links Irvine, Kilwinning and Eglinton Country Park.

GO FORTH ON CYCLES – KINCARDINE TO LIMEKILNS

This is a good, interesting and varied coastal route, which leads by a string of pretty towns to end in the picture-postcard village of Limekilns. Half the route follows a traffic-free path, which, in parts, hugs the shoreline, providing perfect cycling for young and old.

The tall chimney stack at Longannet coal-fired power station – one of Europe's largest – draws the eye. It produces a huge quantity of fly ash, some of which is transported by pipe to form Preston Island; a track follows this pipeline, giving easy cycling by the Firth of Forth, where wading birds thrive.

One of the highlights of this trip is a visit to the ancient burgh of Culross. Many of the colourful, stone buildings of this riverside port owe their inspiration to the Netherlands' town of Veere, with which Culross had strong trade links from the 16th century. Then it was a thriving community, developed under the laird, Sir George Bruce, for whom the striking red-tiled Culross Palace was built.

Similarly, nearby Charlestown is linked to one key historical figure, Charles Elgin, who created the planned village in the 1750s. The original layout of the village, built to accommodate workers in the coal and limestone industries, is still visible; from above it spells the letters 'CE'.

The route finishes by pretty Limekilns, a former crossing point on the firth, which features in Robert Louis Stevenson's novel *Kidnapped*.

ROUTE INFORMATION

National Route: 76
Start: East of old Kincardine Bridge.
Finish: Limekilns.
Distance: 12 miles (19.5km).
Grade: Easy.
Surface: Tarmac, with short section of grass.
Hills: Mainly flat, with a few gentle slopes heading out of Kincardine. Steep climb to Crombie.

YOUNG & INEXPERIENCED CYCLISTS

Suitable for young and inexperienced cyclists, providing care is taken on the quiet road sections.

REFRESHMENTS

- Several eateries in Kincardine.
- Bessie Bar Tearoom, Culross.
- Ship Inn, Limekilns.

THINGS TO SEE & DO

- **Devilla Forest, near Kincardine:** prehistoric coffins, stone circles and Roman urns have all been found in this Scots pine forest, which has a number of waymarked walking and cycling trails; www.forestry.gov.uk
- **The Royal Burgh of Culross:** attractive town that looks as though time has stood still; most complete example in Scotland of a burgh of the 17th and 18th centuries; 0844 493 2189; www.nts.org.uk
- **Preston Island, near Culross:** once an island, this wildlife-rich area is now linked to the mainland by reclaimed land; a cycle-friendly path forms a circuit of the 'island'.
- **Torry Bay Local Nature Reserve, near Torryburn:** extensive mudflats, part of a larger area between Longannet Point and Crombie Point, which are of national importance for wading and wintering birds; 01383 725596; www.snh.org.uk
- **Dunfermline Abbey:** built by King David I of

Limekilns beach, on the Fife coastline

Scotland, its foundations go back to 1072, although its origins can be traced to AD 800; the resting place of Robert the Bruce; 01383 724586; www.dunfermlineabbey.co.uk

TRAIN STATIONS

Alloa; Rosyth; Dunfermline; Inverkeithing; North Queensferry.

BIKE HIRE

- Biketrax, Edinburgh: 0131 228 6633; www.biketrax.co.uk
- Cycle Scotland, Edinburgh: 0131 556 5560; www.cyclescotland.co.uk
- Leith Cycle Co, Leith: 0131 467 7775; www.leithcycleco.com

FURTHER INFORMATION

- To view or print National Cycle Network routes, visit www.sustrans.org.uk
- Maps for this area are available to buy from www.sustransshop.co.uk
- For further information on routes in Scotland, visit www.routes2ride.org.uk/scotland
- Fife Tourist Information: 01383 720999 (Dunfermline office); www.visitfife.com
- Scotland Tourist Information: 0845 225 5121; 0131 625 8625; www.visitscotland.com

ROUTE DESCRIPTION

The route starts on a cycle track just to the east of the old Kincardine Bridge. After crossing a

The handsome Town House at Culross

minor road by Inch Farm, it joins a fine cycle track alongside the road to Culross. Further on, the route follows the line of a pipe that runs from Longannet power station, past Culross to Preston Island.

At Preston Island, a footbridge crosses over the railway line. Then there's a short section of road through Newmills and Low Torry before the route turns right onto a great stretch of track by Torry Bay.

A steep climb leads up to Crombie to join a cyclepath before a descent, on a rough road, to Charlestown. The continuation to Limekilns follows Route 76 along the coast road. From there, you could either retrace the route or cycle on to discover historic Dunfermline.

NEARBY CYCLE ROUTES

The Kincardine to Limekilns trail is part of the Round the Forth Route (National Route 76), which currently follows the coast from Berwick-upon-Tweed to Edinburgh, Stirling and Kirkcaldy. In time, it is planned to extend the route round the East Neuk of Fife to St Andrews.

The West Fife Way (Route 764) is an excellent, flat and traffic-free route that follows an old railway line linking Clackmannan with Dunfermline.

The Coast & Castles Route (National Route 1) runs from Newcastle to Aberdeen and can be accessed at Inverkeithing and Dunfermline.

In Devilla Forest, near Kincardine, there are cycle routes that form part of the Kingdom of Fife Millennium Cycleway.

WEST FIFE WAY – ALLOA TO DUNFERMLINE

Pedal away to your heart's content on a quiet traffic-free route – the West Fife Way – that follows the course of the former Dunfermline to Alloa Railway. The cycleway heads over open and wooded country, passing close by the villages of Blairhall, Oakley and Carnock, which all offer refreshments.

Starting from Alloa train station provides an environmentally friendly way to access the route, while allowing a visit to the impressive Alloa Tower. Clackmannanshire was a sought-after location for medieval aristocrats who commuted to Stirling Castle; there are four medieval tower houses and a manor house within the county's boundaries. Former home to the Erskine family, the Earls of Mar, Alloa Tower is one of the finest of its type in Scotland.

There is also the option of diverting to the mountain bike tracks in Devilla Forest, or onto minor roads to join National Route 76 by the Forth Estuary (see page 66). Look out for the Kingdom of Fife Millennium Cycleway signs with the green diamond; these mark where the Dunfermline–Charlestown–Limekilns and the Cairneyhill–Crossford–Crombie routes meet the cycleway. Both these routes will take you down to the coast.

Dunfermline itself is an attractive and very ancient Scottish town that is worth exploring at leisure.

ROUTE INFORMATION
National Route: 764
Start: Alloa train station.
Finish: Dunfermline Queen Margaret train station.
Distance: 16 miles (26km).
Grade: Easy.
Surface: Tarmac.
Hills: None.

YOUNG & INEXPERIENCED CYCLISTS
The traffic-free cyclepath section from Clackmannan to Dunfermline is ideal for novices and children. Care needs to be taken on the on-road sections that link with train stations at either end, and on the mile-long section through Clackmannan.

REFRESHMENTS
- Lots of choice in Alloa and Dunfermline.
- Pubs and shop in Clackmannan.
- Various options in the villages of Blairhall, Oakley and Carnock.

THINGS TO SEE & DO
- **Alloa Tower:** ancestral home of the Earls of Mar, this is one of Scotland's largest surviving medieval tower houses, with an important collection of portraits; 0844 493 2129; www.nts.org.uk
- **Clackmannan Tower:** a fine 14th-century keep, enlarged in the 15th century, which was granted to Robert the Bruce; enjoys excellent views of the River Forth; interior viewing only on certain occasions; 01786 431326; www.historic-scotland.gov.uk
- **Devilla Forest, east of Clackmannan:** prehistoric coffins, stone circles and Roman urns have all been found in this predominantly Scots pine forest; there are a number of waymarked walking and cycling trails; www.forestry.gov.uk
- **Dunfermline Abbey:** built by King David I of Scotland; its foundations go back to 1072, although its origins can be traced to AD 800; the resting place of Robert the Bruce; 01383 724586; www.dunfermlineabbey.co.uk

Alloa Tower in winter

TRAIN STATIONS
Alloa; DunfermlineTown; Dunfermline Queen Margaret.

BIKE HIRE
- **Biketrax, Edinburgh:** 0131 228 6633; www.biketrax.co.uk
- **Cycle Scotland, Edinburgh:** 0131 556 5560; www.cyclescotland.co.uk
- **Leith Cycle Co, Leith:** 0131 467 7775; www.leithcycleco.com

FURTHER INFORMATION
- To view or print National Cycle Network routes, visit www.sustrans.org.uk
- Maps for this area are available to buy from www.sustransshop.co.uk
- For further information on routes in Scotland, visit www.routes2ride.org.uk/scotland
- **Fife Tourist Information:** 01383 720999; www.visitfife.com
- **Scotland Tourist Information:** 0845 225 5121; 0131 625 8625; www.visitscotland.com

ROUTE DESCRIPTION
From Alloa train station, follow the signs for the town centre, which direct you up Primrose Street. Go left at the top and first right, right again at the T-junction with Mill Street and then first left onto Mar Street. Follow this past Candleriggs car park. The imposing Alloa Tower, on Route 76, is straight ahead. Cycle to the right and round the tower to pick up the route to Dunfermline. The route follows traffic-free paths and residential roads before

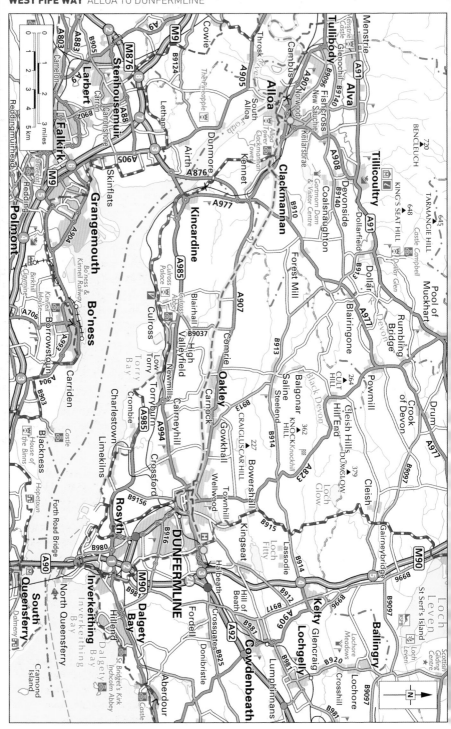

Stained glass in
Dunfermline Abbey

crossing a road and turning left onto an excellent traffic-free section through woods.

This joins the busy B910, which leads into Clackmannan. Follow this road for 1 mile (1.6km) to join the signed West Fife Path via a ramp. The ride then follows an old railway line, providing safe and pleasurable cycling, to reach the western outskirts of Dunfermline. From there, follow the Kingdom of Fife Millennium Cycleway signs that lead via Golfrum Street, Campbell Street, Leys Park Road and a cyclepath to Dunfermline Queen Margaret station.

NEARBY CYCLE ROUTES

The Alloa to Clackmannan section of the West Fife Way is shared with the Round the Forth Route (National Route 76), which currently follows the coast from Berwick-upon-Tweed to Edinburgh, Stirling and Kirkcaldy. In time, it is planned to extend the route round the East Neuk of Fife to St Andrews.

The Coast & Castles Route (National Route 1), which runs from Newcastle to Aberdeen, can be accessed at Dunfermline Queen Margaret train station.

Cycle routes in Devilla Forest, east of Clackmannan, form part of the Kingdom of Fife Millennium Cycleway. The forest entrance is adjacent to, and signed from, the West Fife Way.

The Kingdom of Fife Millennium Cycleway is made up of 300 miles (500km) of cycle routes. The traffic-free routes, in particular, are recommended. Maps are available from: www.fifedirect.org.uk/fife-cycleways

FOREST & LOCH – ABERFOYLE TO CALLANDER

A beautiful forest, mountain views and a peaceful loch are all waiting to be explored on the superb Forest & Loch Route in the heart of the Trossachs. The concept of tourism was established here in Victorian times, and when you come you'll see why the travelling masses were smitten.

Cyclewise, it's a route of two halves. It begins with a bang – a stiff initial climb from the town of Aberfoyle, which is best enjoyed by fit riders, to an airy spot by a lochan. The reward is a fun, pine-scented, descent to picturesque Loch Venachar. The lochshore trail here is among the best in the country and is ideal for all the family. It passes a host of perfect picnic spots.

Further on, a minor road is followed, which runs by the loch with views of shapely Ben Ledi. Along the way, the route also passes the Menteith Hills. These low-lying hills have an important geological story to tell: they mark the Highland Boundary Fault. This ancient fault line divides the Lowlands from the Highlands, once separate landmasses, which remain disparate to this day.

From the end of the loch the bustling town of Callander is easily reached, where hungry cyclists will find everything they need to refuel and relax.

ROUTE INFORMATION

National Route: 7
Start: Main Street, Aberfoyle.
Finish: Callander Meadows, centre of Callander.
Distance: 13 miles (21km).
Grade: Challenging.
Surface: Tarmac, forest road, forest track.
Hills: Very steep climb from the start for 2 miles (3km), followed by a descent and a level lochshore section.

YOUNG & INEXPERIENCED CYCLISTS

Due to the steep start, novices and children are advised to follow the section from Callander to the end of Loch Venachar; this has a superb 2-mile (3km) traffic-free section west of Invertrossachs.

REFRESHMENTS

- Lots of choice of cafes and food-serving pubs in both Aberfoyle and Callander.
- Bluebell Cafe, David Marshall Lodge, Achray Forest.
- Many picnic spots along the lochshore trail.

Achray Forest and the peak of Ben Ledi

THINGS TO SEE & DO

- David Marshall Lodge Visitor Centre, Achray Forest, near Aberfoyle: forest walks and wildlife viewing (osprey, red squirrel), aerial assault course and children's play area; 01877 382383; www.forestry.gov.uk
- Faery Hill, near Aberfoyle: it's a short, popular walk to this hill, said to harbour fairies and the spirit of a curious minister; www.visitscottishheartlands.com
- The Hamilton Toy Collection, Callander: toys from the last 100 years; also has a well-stocked shop; 01877 330004; www.thehamiltontoycollection.co.uk
- *Sir Walter Scott* steamship, Loch Katrine: plying the loch since 1899, this converted steamship adds a touch of Victorian drama to a trip on the beautiful Trossachs loch; bicycles carried – ideal for a return by the 11-mile (17.5km) lochshore cyclepath; 01877 332000; www.lochkatrine.com

TRAIN STATIONS

Dunblane: Follow roads, some busy, to Callander, approximately 11 miles (17.5km). Not recommended for novices or families.

BUSES

Trossachs Trundler Bus can take up to two bikes from Stirling bus station to Callander (summer only); 01786 442707

BIKE HIRE

- Trossachs Holiday Park, 3 miles (5km) south of Aberfoyle on A81: 01877 382614; www.trossachsholidays.co.uk

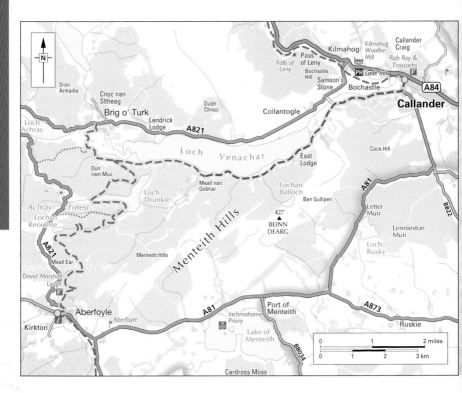

- Wheels Cycling Centre, Callander:
  01877 331100; www.scottish-cycling.com

FURTHER INFORMATION

- To view or print National Cycle Network
  routes, visit www.sustrans.org.uk
- Maps for this area are available to buy from
  www.sustransshop.co.uk
- For more information on routes in Scotland,
  visit www.routes2ride.org.uk/scotland
- Trossachs Discovery Centre, Aberfoyle:
  01877 382352;
  www.visitscottishheartlands.com
- Scotland Tourist Information: 0845 225 5121;
  0131 625 8625; www.visitscotland.com

ROUTE DESCRIPTION

From the Trossach's gateway town of
Aberfoyle, the route climbs very steeply for

500m (1,640ft) up the A821. The gradient eases
as the route leaves the road to follow a forest
track (follow Route 7 signs). A short diversion
leads to the signed visitor centre.

The ride continues past the Little Fawn
Waterfall. Turn right to resume climbing a wide
forest road (mountain bikes or hybrids
recommended), reaching a height of 280m
(920ft), followed by a long downhill stretch to
Loch Venachar on forest roads. Cars follow part
of this section as a one-way forest drive, though
traffic is light and there is a low speed limit.

The route continues past Loch Drunkie
before a fast descent leading past a car park.
Just before the forest road levels, Route 7 signs
indicate a sharp turn to the right towards Loch
Venachar. (An excursion to Loch Katrine can be
followed by going straight ahead and then by
the south side of Loch Achray. You can also

Ben Ledi towers beyond
Callander's main street

Highland cow

divert from the sharp turn to reach a welcoming pub near Brig o'Turk.) A delightful forest track leads to Loch Venachar. After 2 miles (3km) this joins a minor road leading to Callander.

NEARBY CYCLE ROUTES

The Forest & Loch Route is part of the Lochs &

Glens Route (National Route 7) – a 429-mile (690km) epic ride from Carlisle to Inverness.

The Loch Katrine cyclepath, one of Scotland's finest, is traffic-free and can be followed for 11 miles (17.5km). Loch Katrine, 4 miles (6.5km) from the Forest & Loch Route, can be accessed from forest tracks and roads.

ROB ROY COUNTRY – CALLANDER TO KILLIN

Callander lies just south of Highland Perthshire. It was created as a 'new town' in the 1730s by the Duke of Perth, and in the late 18th century it was a thriving centre for weaving. In Victorian times, it became a popular spa town due to its location close to the Trossachs and its association with the novels of Sir Walter Scott. A railway branch line from Dunblane was built in 1858, and the line was later extended to Crianlarich and Oban. The town featured in the 1960s television series *Dr Finlay's Casebook* as Tannochbrae.

You should enjoy spectacular views of Ben Ledi (876m/2,874ft) and Loch Lubnaig along the course of the dismantled railway linking Callander with Strathyre via the Falls of Leny and the west side of Loch Lubnaig. It is said that 2,000 years ago the Druids lit fires at the top of Ben Ledi to celebrate the changing of the seasons.

Rob Roy MacGregor (1671–1734) was an outlaw and Scottish folk hero, sometimes known as the Scottish Robin Hood. Celebrated in the novel *Rob Roy* by Sir Walter Scott, he lived his last years in Balquhidder. He and other members of the MacGregor clan are buried in the churchyard; his grave is marked by a slate slab carved with a kilted figure.

Buildings in Callander

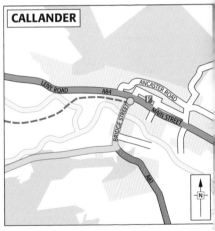

ROUTE INFORMATION

National Route: 7
Start: Callander Meadows, centre of Callander.
Finish: Killin, Balquhidder or Brig O'Turk.
Distance: Callander to Killin 25 miles (40km);
Callander to Balquhidder 13 miles (21km);
Callander to Brig o'Turk 8 miles (13km).
Grade: Moderate to difficult.
Surface: Mixture of tarmac and stone-based tracks. There are rougher sections at the north end of Loch Lubnaig and going into Killin.
Hills: The route has a number of hills, including:

- a steady 61m (200ft) climb from Callander, past the Falls of Leny, up to Loch Lubnaig
- a steep hill at the north end of Loch Lubnaig (fantastic views!)
- a very steep climb from Lochearnhead to Glen Ogle.

- a steep descent from Glenoglehead towards Killin.

YOUNG & INEXPERIENCED CYCLISTS

Callander to Killin: The route is mainly made up of traffic-free paths and quiet roads. There can be considerable holiday traffic between Balquhidder and Kingshouse. Take extreme

The Falls of Dochart

care crossing the trunk road at Glenoglehead.
Callander to Brig O'Turk: There is a short
section (0.25 mile/0.4km) on the A81 south from
the centre of Callander, where care should be
taken. The rest of the route is on minor roads
and cyclepaths.

REFRESHMENTS
- Lots of choice in Callander.
- Cafe and pubs in Strathyre.
- Teashop at the museum in Stronvar, just
  south of Balquhidder.
- Lots of choice in Lochearnhead.
- Lots of choice in Killin.

THINGS TO SEE & DO
- The Hamilton Toy Collection: a celebration of
  toys from the last hundred years; 01877
  330004; www.thehamiltontoycollection.co.uk
- **Kilmahog & Trossachs Mills:** traditional
  Scottish knitwear, plus country and outdoor
  clothing; 01877 330178;
  www.trossachswoollenmill.com
- **Falls of Leny and Pass of Leny:** beautiful
  waterfalls surrounded by woodland;
  www.visitscotland.com
- **Loch Lubnaig:** loch near Callander.
- **Glen Ogle:** spectacular pass with views of
  Loch Earn.
- **Rob Roy's grave, Balquhidder:** grave of the
  famous Scottish folk hero of the early 18th
  century, Rob Roy MacGregor, situated in
  Balquhidder's parish church;
  www.undiscoveredscotland.co.uk
- **Falls of Dochart, Killin:** series of rapids that
  carry the River Dochart through the village.

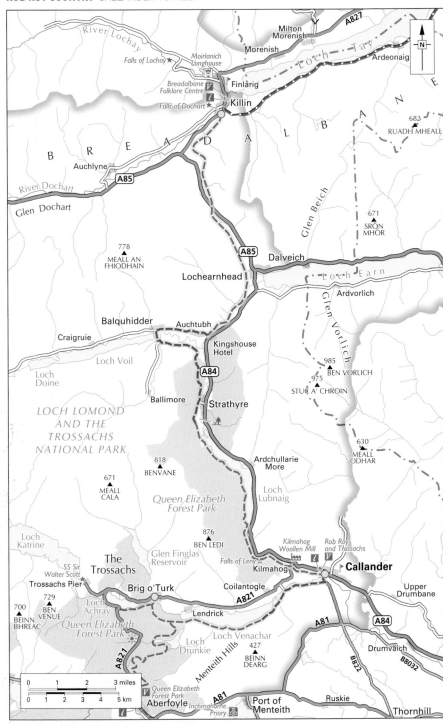

TRAIN STATIONS

Dunblane: Follow roads, some busy, to
Callander, approximately 11 miles (17.5km).
Not recommended for novices or families.

BUSES

Trossachs Trundler Bus can take up to two
bikes from Stirling bus station to Callander
(summer only); 01786 442707

BIKE HIRE

- Mounter Bikes (Cycle Hire), Callander: 01877
  331052; www.callandercyclehire.co.uk
- Killin Outdoor Centre: 01567 820652;
  www.killinoutdoor.co.uk

FURTHER INFORMATION

- To view or print National Cycle Network
  routes, visit www.sustrans.org.uk
- Maps for this area are available to buy from
  www.sustransshop.co.uk
- For more information on routes in Scotland,
  visit www.routes2ride.org.uk/scotland
- Scotland Tourist Information: 0845 225 5121;
  0131 625 8625; www.visitscotland.com

ROUTE DESCRIPTION

The route travels north to Balquhidder along
the course of the old Caledonian railway line.
Passing through woodland, alongside the swift
waters and spectacular falls of the River Leny,
you cycle through the Pass of Leny. It then
follows the shores of Loch Lubnaig. Please note
that halfway along there is a short section of
zigzag slopes and rough surfaces.

At the end of Loch Lubnaig, the route takes
a quiet road to Balquhidder, where you can visit
Rob Roy's grave. From here, you can continue
through the spectacular Glen Ogle, once
described by Queen Victoria as Scotland's
Khyber Pass, with some excellent views of Loch
Earn, to make your way to Killin and Loch Tay.
This section of the route uses the old military
road, two railway paths and two listed viaducts.
A shorter ride from Callander to Brig o'Turk

follows a quiet road and cycle track along the
shores of Loch Venachar, passing splendid
isolated houses set above the water's edge
and offering views across to Ben Ledi. The
loch ends at Blackwater Marshes. You then
follow a short section on forest roads to reach
the refreshment stop/turnaround point at Brig
o'Turk.

NEARBY CYCLE ROUTES

From Killin, National Route 7 continues to Loch
Tay, Pitlochry, Aviemore, and Inverness. To the
south of Loch Venachar, Route 7 crosses the
Dukes Pass via forestry tracks (see page 74),
then passes through Aberfoyle and Drymen on
its way to Loch Lomond and Glasgow.

There are plenty of forest routes in the
Queen Elizabeth Forest Park. There is also a
delightful ride on a traffic-free Scottish Water
road along the northern side of Loch Katrine to
Stronachlachar, which can be continued on
minor roads to Loch Lomond or Aberfoyle.

Crossing Glen Ogle Viaduct

UP THE TAY – PERTH TO DUNKELD

Follow the mighty Tay, Scotland's longest river, from the attractive town of Perth to historic Dunkeld in Highland Perthshire. This gentle cycle ride is ideal for a relaxing outing – there are few hills and, if you wish, you can return to the start by train.

Part of the Salmon Run route, this trip gives unrivalled views of the prestigious fishing river that flows grandly by wood-lined banks. It carries an awful lot of water, draining more land than any other British river. The Tay's banks are also soaked in history.

Upriver from Perth, Scone Palace sits by one of Scotland's most important historic centres, where the kings of the country were crowned on the Stone of Destiny. The flat cyclepath affords views of the rebuilt Scone Palace – a late Georgian Gothic house, which can be seen on the opposite side of the river.

The route then follows the River Almond until it heads away to climb to pretty Pitcairngreen on minor roads, before joining a short section of cyclepath that leads through the Pass of Birnam and Birnam Wood. The latter, of course, features in Shakespeare's *Macbeth* and is a delight at any time of year. After crossing the Tay on a grand Telford-designed bridge, you enter Dunkeld, where there is a fine music pub by the river and other attractions. An optional, and highly recommended detour, is to continue on the traffic-free route that leads upstream through the grounds of a country house hotel.

ROUTE INFORMATION
National Route: 77
Start: North Inch, Perth.
Finish: Dunkeld & Birnam train station.
Distance: 17 miles (27.5km).
Grade: Easy.
Surface: Tarmac and gravel.
Hills: Rolling, except for some short but steep climbs near Pitcairngreen.

YOUNG & INEXPERIENCED CYCLISTS
The roads are mainly quiet but, as ever, vigilance is required.

REFRESHMENTS
- No 1 The Bank restaurant, Perth.
- Caffe Nero, Perth.
- The Pitcairngreen Inn, Pitcairngreen.
- The Taybank pub, Dunkeld.
- Katie's Tearoom, Dunkeld.

THINGS TO SEE & DO
- Scone Palace, Old Scone, near Perth: rightful home of the Stone of Destiny, Scone was

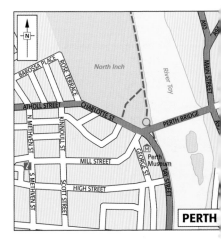

where Scots kings were crowned from the ninth to the 17th century; the palace has a fine collection of antiques and paintings and an impressive arboretum; 01738 552300; www.scone-palace.co.uk
- Scottish Liqueur Centre, Bankfoot: learn more about the traditions of distilling

The River Tay at Dunkeld

The remains of the cathedral at Dunkeld

liqueurs and whiskies at the visitor centre; 01738 787044; www.scottish-liqueur-centre.com

- **Beatrix Potter Exhibition, Birnam Institute, Birnam:** the much-loved author Beatrix Potter spent her childhood summers in the area, which directly inspired such classics as *The Tale of Jeremy Fisher*; young and old will enjoy the exhibition and adjacent garden; 01350 727674; www.birnaminstitute.com
- **Dunkeld Cathedral:** part ruin and part parish church, the cathedral is situated in an enviable position overlooking the Tay; it features the tomb of the infamous 'Wolf of Badenoch'; www.dunkeldcathedral.org.uk

TRAIN STATIONS
Perth; Dunkeld & Birnam.

BIKE HIRE
- **Perth City Cycles:** 01738 639346; www.perthcitycycles.co.uk
- **Escape Route, Pitlochry:** 01796 473859; www.escape-route.biz

FURTHER INFORMATION
- To view or print National Cycle Network routes, visit www.sustrans.org.uk
- Maps for this area are available to buy from www.sustransshop.co.uk
- For further information on routes in Scotland, visit www.routes2ride.org.uk/scotland
- **Perthshire Tourist Information:** 0845 225 5121; 01506 832121; www.perthshire.co.uk
- **Scotland Tourist Information:** 0845 225 5121; 0131 625 8625; www.visitscotland.com

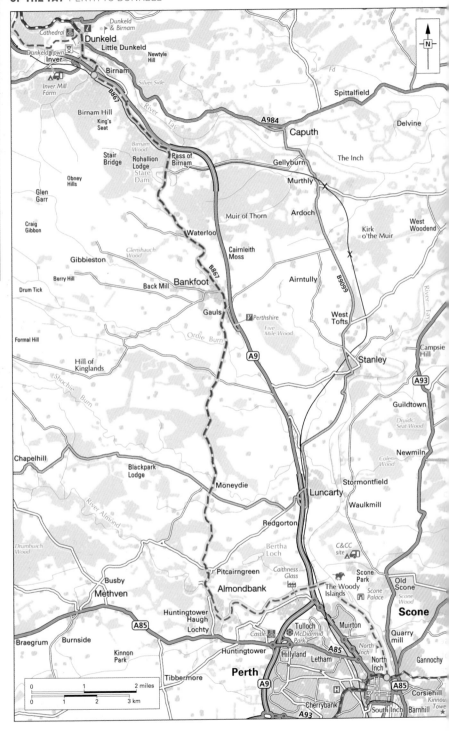

Scone Palace

ROUTE DESCRIPTION

In Perth, the route runs through the broad
parkland of North Inch and continues on a level
traffic-free path alongside the River Tay for just
over 2 miles (3km), before following the course
of the River Almond to Almondbank. Minor
roads are then followed for the majority of the
ride, via Pitcairngreen, Moneydie and Bankfoot,
before a mile-long section of cyclepath (near
the A9) leads through the Pass of Birnam,
ending at Dunkeld & Birnam train station.

The twin towns of Dunkeld and Birnam are
separated by the River Tay. Dunkeld, the larger
of the two, is well worth a visit. From there, you
can follow a beautiful stretch of the river on a
traffic-free path, accessed via the Hilton
Dunkeld House Hotel. This traffic-free section
of National Route 77 can be followed for 2 miles

(3km) to a bridge on the A9, after which it
continues north on-road.

NEARBY CYCLE ROUTES

The Perth to Dundee trail is part of the longer
54-mile (87km) Salmon Run (National Route
77), which runs from Dundee to Pitlochry.

National Route 77 meets National Route 1
at the Tay Road Bridge in Dundee. Part of the
North Sea Cycle Route, Route 1 runs north to
John o'Groats, Orkney and Shetland or south to
Edinburgh and beyond. National Route 77 also
joins National Route 7 north of Dunkeld at
Ballinluig. Known as the Lochs & Glens route, it
leads north to Inverness and south to Carlisle.

Waymarked mountain bike trails are found at
the Forestry Commission's Kinnoull Hill, near
Perth, and Craigvinean Forest, near Dunkeld.

SEAFARING HISTORY – ROUTES OUT OF DUNDEE

Dundee is Scotland's fourth largest city, with a proud history of seafaring. The town grew rapidly during the Industrial Revolution as a trading centre for the British Empire and a manufacturing centre for flax and jute. The latter was imported from India and the whale oil needed for its processing came from the city's large whaling industry. Next to the award-winning Discovery Point Visitor Centre, you can visit RRS *Discovery*, Captain Scott's Antarctic expedition ship, which was built in Dundee. Also worth a visit are the Sensation Science Centre and the Verdant Works, a restored jute mill and museum.

Broughty Castle, dating from the 15th century and restored in 1860, is situated on an outcrop of rock above Broughty Ferry Harbour. It now houses a museum with displays on the life and times of Broughty Ferry, its people, the local environment and wildlife.

To the southeast of Tayport, Tentsmuir Forest is an open mature pine forest next to a vast expanse of sandy beaches and the Tentsmuir Point National Nature Reserve. The area is criss-crossed with easy, waymarked, off-road cycle routes. The Tay Estuary forms an important feeding and roosting area for seabirds, as well as a haul-out area for common and grey seals.

ROUTE INFORMATION

National Route: 1
Start: Cycle lane access point at the northern end of the Tay Road Bridge, Dundee.
Finish: Tayport, Carnoustie or Arbroath.
Distance: Dundee to Tayport 3.5 miles (5.5km); Dundee to Carnoustie 11 miles (17.5km); Dundee to Arbroath 19 miles (30.5km).
Grade: Easy.
Surface: Tarmac.
Hills: A noticeable climb on the return leg from Tayport up to the southern end of the Tay Bridge. At the northern end of the bridge, a lift takes you from street level up to the central cycle lane.

YOUNG & INEXPERIENCED CYCLISTS

Dundee to Tayport: Excellent traffic-free path running along the middle of the bridge, followed by shared-use route and railway path. No busy roads but care should be taken at crossings and at points with minimal traffic.
Dundee to Arbroath via Carnoustie: a combination of segregated cyclepaths through Dundee docks, quiet roads and traffic-free cycle routes.

REFRESHMENTS

- Lots of choice in Dundee, Carnoustie and Arbroath.
- Cafe/kiosk in the car park at the southern end of the Tay Road Bridge.
- Jane's Harbour Tearoom and Bell Rock Tavern in Tayport.
- Ship Inn, Broughty Ferry.

THINGS TO SEE & DO

- Firth of Tay.
- Tay Road Bridge.
- Discovery Point, Discovery Quay: home of RRS *Discovery*, the ship that took Captain Scott on his first expedition to Antarctica, and Verdant Works, a restored jute mill; 01382 309060; www.rrsdiscovery.com
- HM Frigate *Unicorn*, Victoria Dock: wooden warship launched in 1824; 01382 200900; www.frigateunicorn.org
- Sensation Science Centre: pioneering science museum for adults and children; 01382 228800; www.sensation.org.uk
- Claypotts Castle, near Dundee: well-preserved 16th-century castle; external viewing only; 01786 431324; www.historic-scotland.gov.uk

Dundee city centre and the River Tay

DUNDEE

- Signal Tower Museum, Arbroath: covers the history of the Bell Rock lighthouse and shore station, and houses the massive lens of the last manually operated lamp; 01241 435329; www.angus.gov.uk/history/museums
- Arbroath Abbey: beautiful ruin, founded in 1178; 01241 878756; www.historic-scotland.gov.uk

TRAIN STATIONS
Dundee; Broughty Ferry; Balmossie; Monifieth; Barry Links; Golf Street; Carnoustie; Arbroath.

- Broughty Castle and Museum: originally built in the late 15th century, with stunning views over the Tay; the museum tells the story of Broughty Ferry and the local area; 01382 436916; www.historic-scotland.gov.uk

BIKE HIRE
- Cycle World Bike Hire Centre, Arbroath: 01241 876034; www.cycle-world.co.uk

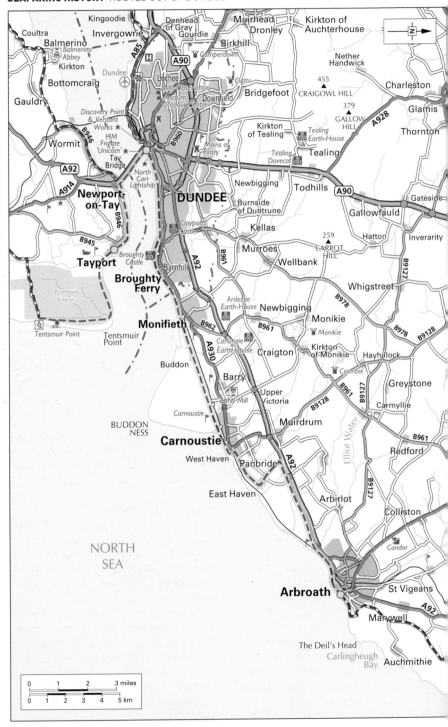

FURTHER INFORMATION

- To view or print National Cycle Network routes, visit www.sustrans.org.uk
- Maps for this area are available to buy from www.sustransshop.co.uk
- For more information on routes in Scotland, visit www.routes2ride.org.uk/scotland
- **Dundee Tourist Information:** 01382 527527; www.angusanddundee.co.uk
- **Scotland Tourist Information:** 0845 225 5121; 0131 625 8625; www.visitscotland.com

ROUTE DESCRIPTION

Heading towards Tayport from the Dundee side of the Tay Road Bridge, you access the bridge by lift. Cross the bridge on a central elevated cyclepath, which gives great views in both directions along the Firth of Tay. There is a descent from the bridge before joining a railway path that runs along the southern shore of the Firth of Tay to the harbourside in Tayport. If you are feeling particularly energetic, you can continue on Route 1 into Tentsmuir Forest and explore the delightful waymarked woodland tracks that form part of the Kingdom of Fife Millennium Cycleway.

Heading towards Carnoustie and Arbroath, go through the Dundee port area – you will be asked for photo ID. To date, there is no access for pedestrians through the port. If you are not granted access, there is an alternative route on public roads; see map on page 87. On busy roads you may want to push your bike along the pavement.

Beyond the docks, the route follows the shoreline on a fine promenade path and Broughty Castle comes into view. It then runs close to the sea to Monifieth, from where a well-maintained cyclepath heads over Barry Links. Carnoustie offers opportunities for refreshments and a view of the famous championship golf course. The route continues on the cyclepath to East Haven, where it heads inland on a farm road and then turns towards Arbroath on a cycleway alongside the A92. You

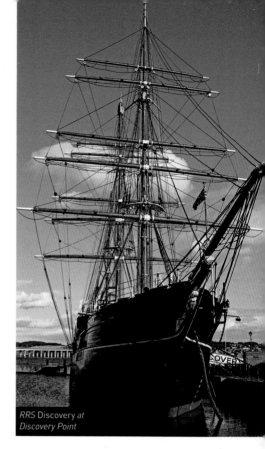

RRS Discovery *at Discovery Point*

can ride the route in either direction and make your return journey by bike or train. For a shorter ride, you can catch a train from one of the railway stations along the route.

NEARBY CYCLE ROUTES

The ride forms part of National Route 1, which crosses Fife from Edinburgh, then passes through Dundee on its way up the east coast to Aberdeen, Inverness and John o'Groats.

National Route 77 heads west from Dundee to Perth and north to Pitlochry.

There are easy, waymarked traffic-free trails in Tentsmuir Forest, to the southeast of Tayport, which can be accessed by following Route 1 beyond the end of this ride towards Leuchars and St Andrews.

There are three other forests in Fife that have waymarked trails: Pitmedden, Devilla and Blairadam.

THE CALEDONIA WAY

Since 2007 Sustrans and its partners have been creating a traffic-free cycling route between Oban and Fort William. Much of the path between Oban and Ballachulish is now complete, giving safe cycling access to some of the most stunning scenery in Britain, along a route peppered with fantastic places to visit. The path has been built along the former railway line which ran from Connel to the slate quarries near Ballachulish and closed in 1966. Some of the old line was used to improve the A828 trunk road; however, substantial sections of the disused railway remain and are being used for this traffic-free path. Work on the route continues, with the intention to complete the whole route by 2014. All the completed sections are described here. Where no traffic-free path has yet been built, the only alternative may be the A828, which is not suitable for all cycling abilities. North of Ballachulish the long-term aim is to build a path along the east shore of Loch Linnhe, but for now we recommend cyclists use the Corran ferry, cycle up the west shore of the loch and cross to Fort William on the Camusnagaul ferry. When complete, the Oban to Fort William route will be 46 miles (74km) long. It will become part of Route 78 of the National Cycle Network, running from Campbeltown all the way to Inverness, 228 miles (367km) in total, which will be known as the Caledonia Way (Slighe na h-Alba).

ROUTE INFORMATION
Start: Oban station.
Finish: South Ballachulish.
Distance: 33 miles (53km).
Grade: Medium.
Surface: Well-surfaced cyclepaths and roads.
Hills: Although the region is mountainous, the road follows the side of the numerous lochs to make it the flattest route possible with few hills.

Along the Oban to Connel section

YOUNG & INEXPERIENCED CYCLISTS
The traffic-free sections are a great place for children and novices. The sections along the A828 may not suit cyclists of all abilities.

REFRESHMENTS
- Plenty of places in Oban and in the Ballachulish area, where seafood is a speciality.

There is also:
- The Wide Mouthed Frog, Dunstaffnage Marina.
- The Oyster Inn, Connel.
- Ben Lora Cafe, Benderloch.
- The Twisted Wheel Cafe, between Benderloch and Barcaldine.
- Scottish Sea Life Sanctuary, Barcaldine.
- Holly Tree Hotel, Kentallen.
- Shops at Benderloch and Duror.

THINGS TO SEE & DO
- McCaig's Tower, Oban.
- Cathedral of St Columba in Oban: www.rcdai.org.uk/cathedral.html
- Oban Distillery: 01631 572004; www.discovering-distilleries.com

- Dunollie Castle: www.dunollie.org
- Dunstaffnage Marina:
  www.dunstaffnagemarina.co.uk
- Kintaline Farm: www.kintaline.co.uk
- Scottish Sea Life Sanctuary: 01631 720386;
  www.sealsanctuary.co.uk/oban1.html
- Kinlochlaich Gardens:
  www.kinlochlaich-house.co.uk
- Castle Stalker: www.castlestalker.com
- Glencoe & North Lorn Folk Museum:
  www.glencoemuseum.com
- Isle of Lismore: www.isleoflismore.com

TRAIN STATIONS
Oban; Connel Ferry.

BIKE HIRE
- Flit Bike Hire, Oban: 01631 566553;
  www.flitselfdrive.co.uk
- Port Appin Bikes, Port Appin: 01631 730391;
  www.portappinbikehire.netfirms.com
- CranKitUpGear, Glencoe: 01855 811694;
  www.crankitupgear.com

- Nevis Cycles, Fort William: 01397 705555;
  wwwfortwilliambikehire.co.uk
- Alpine Bikes, Fort William: 01397 704008;.
  www.alpinebikes.com/shops/fort-william

FURTHER INFORMATION
- To view or print National Cycle Network
  routes, visit www.sustrans.org.uk
- Maps for this area are available to buy from
  www.sustransshop.co.uk (the only map
  available of this route is free at the moment)
- Oban Tourist Information: 01631 563122; `
  www.visitscottishheartlands.com
- Ballachulish Tourist Information:
  01855 811866; www.glencoetourism.co.uk
- Fort William Tourist Information:
  01397 701801; www.visithighlands.com

ROUTE DESCRIPTION
For Oban to Dunbeg, head north out of Oban
along the coast. The road hugs the shore and is
narrow in places. You will pass the Dog Stone
where legend has it that Fingal chained his

Look out for four-legged pedestrians

THE CALEDONIA WAY

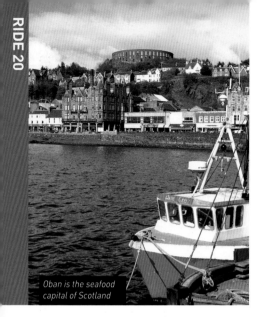
Oban is the seafood capital of Scotland

a 6-mile (9.5km) loop around Loch Creran, and a 10-mile (16km) circuit to Port Appin, where you can take a 10-minute ride on the passenger ferry to the island of Lismore and cycle this 9-mile (14km) island end to end. The main route continues to Dalnatrat, where again you have to join the A828 for 5 miles (8km) to Kentallen, except for a short traffic-free section in Duror. In Kentallen you rejoin a traffic-free path for the final 3 miles (5km) to South Ballachulish. Starting at the Holly Tree Hotel, this is one of the most scenic sections of the route, running along the shore and past the woods of Leitir Mohr, where there is a cairn marking the spot of the notorious shooting of Colin Campbell (known as the Red Fox) in 1752. A short section of the route is on minor roads through Glenachulish, then it's back on the railway path through wooded cuttings to South Ballachulish. From here you can cross the bridge to North Ballachulish or continue to Ballachulish village itself and beyond to Glencoe. At Glencoe you can also join the Loch Leven Loop, a 20-mile (32km) ride all the way back round to North Ballachulish via Kinlochleven, where you can visit the world's largest ice climbing wall or climb up to Grey Mare's Tail waterfall. You will also pass the Loch Leven Seafood Cafe on the north side of the loch, where you can try fresh local produce.

NEARBY CYCLE ROUTES
The route from Oban to Taynuilt follows Glen Lonan – a quiet glen with little traffic on its single-track road. It is great for cycling, but, due to the undulating terrain, best enjoyed by fitter riders. The glen has a long history: from the 9th century Scotland's kings were carried through it on their final journey from the Perthshire palace of Scone to be buried in Iona. After a final climb, the road descends to Taynuilt, whose name is derived from the Gaelic *Tigh-an-Uillt*, meaning 'house of the stream'. The village was a staging post and resting place for travellers before the railway came in 1879.

hunting hound, Bran. Continue under the ivy-clad ruins of Dunollie Castle before reaching the sandy beach at Ganavan. Head from the car park onto the tarmac path which winds for a mile across moorlands to Dunbeg, Dunstaffnage Marina and the ruins of Dunstaffnage Castle. The section of the route to Connel and then parts of the route to Benderloch are currently on the A828, which may not suit cyclists of all abilities. At Benderloch the route joins a traffic-free path alongside the road, and from here you can access the Benderloch Loop, a 4-mile (6.5km) ride that takes in the beautiful sands of Tralee Beach, Kintaline Farm and Barcaldine Castle (private house). The short section of the main route north to Barcaldine is again on the A828, but from here you join the picturesque 13-mile (21km) section of the route from Loch Creran to Loch Linnhe which is almost entirely on traffic-free paths. Head north from the car park at the Scottish Sea Life Sanctuary and follow the cycle route signs. Apart from minor roads in Barcaldine, the path alongside the trunk road between Creagan and Inverfolla and an old road from Dallens to Dalnatrat, the route follows the old railway line. As you head past Appin, look out for a close-up view of Castle Stalker from the shore. This section of the route also boasts

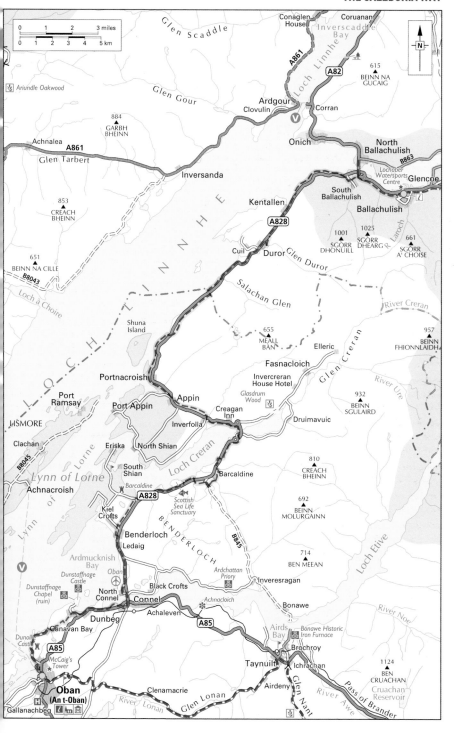

SEAL OF APPROVAL – BARCALDINE TO CREAGAN

This route allows a wonderful opportunity to cycle along a scenic part of the hugely indented west coast of Argyll. The rocky shoreline, with its inaccessible coves and islands, presents ideal habitats for both grey and common seals. Larger animals include basking sharks and dolphins. Otters might also be seen along the shoreline here if you're lucky.

However, you're guaranteed to see North American otters, as well as a range of marine life, at the Scottish Sea Life Sanctuary where the route starts. The tarmac, almost entirely traffic-free path leads cyclists almost effortlessly (if winds are light) up the shores of Loch Creran, along the route of an old railway line and forest trails.

Ultimately, this section will become part of a fabulous new route from Ballachulish to Oban, part of National Route 78. Artwork reflecting the area's rich maritime and Celtic heritage will adorn the route.

The cyclepath ends by Creagan Bridge but the route continues to follow a very quiet minor road, which loops around upper Loch Creran. This is highly recommended, as the upper section of the sea loch nestles beneath the Appin Hills and is very scenic.

ROUTE INFORMATION

National Route: 78
Start and Finish: The Scottish Sea Life Sanctuary, Barcaldine.
Distance: 13 miles (21km).
Grade: Easy to medium.
Surface: Tarmac; one short gravel section south of Barcaldine.
Hills: Mainly flat with some small hills by Loch Creran.

YOUNG & INEXPERIENCED CYCLISTS

The traffic-free cyclepath section is ideal for novices and young families, though care must be taken crossing the A828. The on-road circuit of Loch Creran is also suitable, provided care is taken, as traffic levels are very low.

REFRESHMENTS

- The Scottish Sea Life Sanctuary, Barcaldine.
- The Twisted Wheel Cafe, 0.5 mile (0.8km) west of the Sea Life Sanctuary.
- Creagan Inn, Creagan.
- Castle Stalker View Cafe, Appin.
- The Pierhouse Hotel, Port Appin.

THINGS TO SEE & DO

- **The Scottish Sea Life Sanctuary, Barcaldine:** an aquarium combined with a busy rescue and rehabilitation facility for both common and grey seal pups; visitors can watch the centre's North American otters dive and swim; 01631 720386; www.sealsanctuary.co.uk
- **Castle Stalker, Appin:** perched on a tiny island, this squat, 15th-century tower house commands attention; limited opening times; 01631 740315; www.castlestalker.com
- **Glencoe Visitor Centre:** this National Trust for Scotland visitor centre offers interactive displays and activities that explore the landscape, wildlife and history of dramatic Glencoe; 15 miles (24km) northeast of start; 0844 493 2222; www.glencoe-nts.org.uk
- **Glencoe & North Lorn Folk Museum, Glencoe village:** learn about the history of this remarkable area in traditional, heather-thatched cottages; 01855 811664; www.museumsgalleriesscotland.org.uk

TRAIN STATIONS

None.

Sutherland's Grove, Barcaldine

BIKE HIRE

- Port Appin Bikes:
  www.portappinbikehire.netfirms.com
- RCS Cycles, Glen Lonan: 01866 822736;
  www.rcscycles.co.uk
- Evo Bikes, Oban: www.evobikes.co.uk
- Flit Bike Hire, Oban: 01631 566553;
  www.flitselfdrive.co.uk
- CranKitUpGear, Glencoe: 01885 811694;
  www.crankitupgear.com

A particularly scenic stretch of the route

FURTHER INFORMATION

- To view or print National Cycle Network
  routes, visit www.sustrans.org.uk
- Maps for this area are available to buy from
  www.sustransshop.co.uk
- For further information on routes in
  Scotland, visit

  www.routes2ride.org.uk/scotland
- Scottish Heartlands Tourist Information:
  0870 720 0630;
  www.visitscottishheartlands.com
- Scotland Tourist Information:
  0845 225 5121; 0131 625 8625;
  www.visitscotland.com

Island-bound Castle Stalker on
Loch Laich near Portnacroish

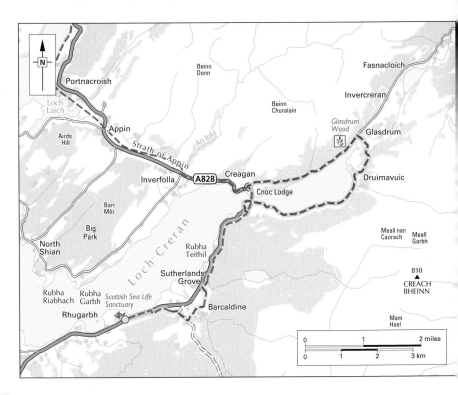

ROUTE DESCRIPTION

The route follows a level, traffic-free, tarmac cyclepath from the northern end of the car park at the Scottish Sea Life Sanctuary, just southwest of Barcaldine. Initially, the path follows the old railway, then the old road, before crossing the A828 and heading to Barcaldine, where minor roads and tracks are followed.

After passing the entrance to an old walled garden (now a camping and caravan site), keep right to reach the path through forested Sutherlands Grove. The path dips down by the A828 before returning to the old railway and leading to a ramp above Creagan Bridge, where there's a fine view.

The Loch Creran circuit is best done clockwise – cross the road, head over the bridge and turn right at the roundabout, signed Invercreran. Follow the minor road by the upper loch, turning right at the junction to return by the southern shore. Further on, the road loops under the A828, where you can rejoin the cyclepath to return to the Scottish Sea Life Sanctuary.

NEARBY CYCLE ROUTES

The Barcaldine to Creagan trail is part of a 32-mile (51.5km) route between Oban and Ballachulish (part of National Route 78) that Sustrans hopes to complete by 2014.

The longer proposed National Route 78 will ultimately extend from Inverness to Campbeltown. The 120-mile (193km) Oban to Campbeltown section is in place, mainly using quiet roads. Cyclists can currently follow the Great Glen from Fort William to Fort Augustus, on the canal towpath and forest roads.

Other sections in place include a tranquil 3-mile (5km) cyclepath that runs southwest from Ballachulish along the old railway line, through the forest and by the coast to the Holly Tree Hotel at Kentallen. North of Oban, a tarmac, traffic-free cyclepath can be followed from Ganavan Sands to Dunbeg for 1.25 miles (2km). The road from Oban to Ganavan leads pleasantly by the ruins of Dunstaffnage Castle. A return circuit to Oban can be made by following the quiet Glencruitten Road, though this involves cycling on the A828 for 1.5 miles (2.5km).

PEDAL HEAVEN – LOCHGILPHEAD TO CRINAN

The shipping shortcut of the west coast, the Crinan Canal is a delight for cyclists of all ages. The canal opened in 1801 to link Ardrishaig Harbour on Loch Fyne with Crinan on the Atlantic. This gave ships an alternative to sailing round the dangerous Mull of Kintyre. The canal is still in use today, though mainly by pleasure boats that ply its dark peaty waters.

A towpath is followed for the entire route, starting from Lochgilphead and leading through lush countryside. At Cairnbaan, you reach the first in a series of locks. To the north of the village lies Kilmartin Glen, which contains hundreds of Cup and Ring marked stones, chambered cairns and stone circles dating from Neolithic/Bronze Age times. You can see a particularly good example of Cup and Ring marked stones just a short distance from the canal at Cairnbaan (a sign points the way). The relevance of these carved markings remains obscure, despite detailed study and discussion by archaeologists.

From Cairnbaan the canal leads by Moine Mhòr (The Great Bog). This is one of the best-preserved and most extensive raised bogs in the UK and has a wild appeal. It is an important breeding ground for osprey, curlew and hen harriers. To the northwest, a small isolated hill, Dunadd, marks the ancient kingdom of the Scotti (so nicknamed by the Romans) – the Irish tribe that settled here from the third century and ultimately united the country, after whom Scotland is named. The top of Dunadd has a foot-shaped hole in which – legend has it – kings placed their foot to become ordained. The route leads easily on to picturesque Crinan, where there is a choice of eateries. Equally easily, from Lochgilphead the canal can also be followed southwards for a mile (1.6km) to pretty Ardrishaig. Those looking for something more strenuous should try the off-road track (a variant of Route 78), which leads south from the village to Inverneill, a distance of some 2 miles (3km).

Crinan Canal

ROUTE INFORMATION

National Route: 78
Start: Seafront at Lochgilphead.
Finish: End of the canal at Crinan.
Distance: 7 miles (11km).
Grade: Easy.
Surface: Stone dust.
Hills: None.

YOUNG & INEXPERIENCED CYCLISTS

This route is ideal for novices and families with young children.

REFRESHMENTS

- Lots of choice in Lochgilphead and Ardrishaig.
- Cairnbaan Hotel, Cairnbaan.
- Crinan Hotel, Crinan.

Crinan Canal at Cairnbaan

- Waterside Cafe, Crinan.

THINGS TO SEE & DO

- **Kilmartin House Museum, Kilmartin:** this award-winning museum is a good starting point for exploring Scotland's richest prehistoric landscape; the glen boasts more than 350 ancient monuments within a 6-mile (9.5km) radius of the village of Kilmartin, 150 of which are prehistoric; 01546 510278; www.kilmartin.org
- **Arduaine Garden, Arduaine:** packed with exotics, such as rhododendrons, azaleas and magnolias, with stunning views overlooking the Sound of Jura; 01852 200366; www.arduaine-garden.org.uk
- **Auchindrain Museum, near Inveraray:** this historic 'farming village' museum allows visitors to step back in time to witness how the local community lived, worked and played; 01499 500235; www.auchindrain-museum.org.uk

TRAIN STATIONS

Oban; Arrochar & Tarbet; Dalmally.

BIKE HIRE

- **Crinan Cycles, Lochgilphead:** 01546 603511; www.crinancycles.co.uk

FURTHER INFORMATION

- To view or print National Cycle Network routes, visit www.sustrans.org.uk
- Maps for this area are available to buy from www.sustransshop.co.uk
- For further information on routes in

*Temple Wood
Standing Stones*

Scotland, visit
www.routes2ride.org.uk/scotland
- For further information on cycle trails in the area (detailed below), visit www.forestry.gov.uk
- Scottish Heartlands Tourist Information: 0870 720 0618;

www.visitscottishheartlands.com
- Scotland Tourist Information: 0845 225 5121; 0131 625 8625; www.visitscotland.com

ROUTE DESCRIPTION

The route is very easy to follow. From

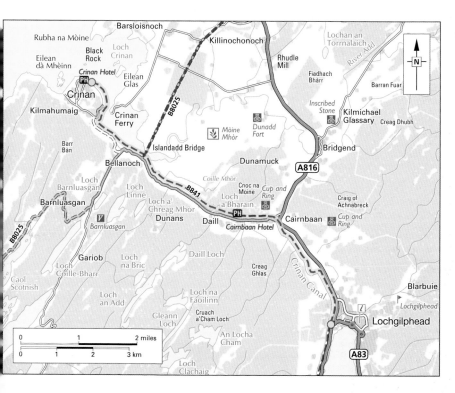

Lochgilphead cycle, or walk, by the main road that runs along the seafront (A83). Turn left at the junction, signed Campbeltown. You will see the raised canal bank ahead, which is reached by a ramp. Turn right along the towpath for Crinan, or left for Ardrishaig.

NEARBY CYCLE ROUTES

The Lochgilphead to Crinan trail is part of the 120-mile (193km) National Route 78 Oban to Campbeltown trail. This will become part of the proposed National Route 78, which will extend from Campbeltown to Inverness. Traffic-free sections are in place between Ganavan and Dunbeg, the Sea Life Sanctuary and Dalnatrat, and Ballachulish and Kentallen. There is a section of quiet road from North Connel and cycle track in Duror. Cyclists can use the canal towpath and forest roads from Fort William to Fort Augustus (see page 102). The Kilmartin Circuit is a circular 20-mile (32km) route, which goes through Kilmartin Glen, famous for its stone circles, standing stones and cairns. From Kilmartin village, it follows Route 78 along the Moine Mhòr and Crinan Canal, via Bridgend, Kilmichael Glassary and Loch Leathan, to rejoin Route 78 south of Ford and return to Kilmartin.

The Firetower Trail, at Achnabreac near Cairnbaan, offers fabulous mountain biking on Forestry Commission land. The routes available are graded blue, red and black. There is something for everyone, though the bulk of the trails are red-graded, with big climbs.

The Faery Isles Cycle Trail (Forestry Commission cycle route) is perfect for all the family, offering a waymarked 12-mile (19.5km) return trip to the remote Starfish Bay from Oib Gate in Knapdale Forest.

GREAT GLEN GETAWAY – FORT WILLIAM TO LAGGAN LOCKS

Billed as 'The Outdoor Capital of the UK', Fort William makes a fantastic base for anyone hooked on the great outdoors. The old garrison town sits by the head of Loch Linnhe, from which the Great Glen extends in a ruler-straight line to Inverness. Through this runs the Caledonian Canal, linking the west coast town with Inverness via a series of lochs and 22 miles (35.5km) of canal. There is excellent family-friendly cycling to be enjoyed alongside the canal and many of the lochs.

This route leads swiftly away from the town on a cyclepath to reach the quiet environs of the 13th-century ruined Inverlochy Castle. In 1307, Robert the Bruce ousted the Comyns from their fortress, ending their threat to his royal ambitions.

From there the route rounds the head of Loch Linnhe, where it joins the end of the Caledonian Canal. Soon after, it reaches Neptune's Staircase – a photogenic flight of eight locks, which raises vessels to 21m (69ft) above sea level. From here there are excellent views of the mighty Ben Nevis.

The towpath runs easily along the canal to the Gairlochy swing bridge. A quiet road then leads to Clunes and an off-road track that runs the length of the unimaginatively titled Loch Lochy. Here you can unwind and ponder the natural forces that tore the country apart to form the Great Glen fault we see today.

ROUTE INFORMATION
National Route: Part of the proposed Route 78
Start: Fort William train station.
Finish: Laggan Locks.
Distance: 22 miles (35.5km).
Grade: Easy.
Surface: Stone dust, tarmac, stony track.
Hills: None.

YOUNG & INEXPERIENCED CYCLISTS
The majority of the route follows traffic-free cyclepaths. Caution needs to be taken on the short, on-road cyclepath sections between Fort William and Corpach (where the towpath is joined) and on the 4-mile (6.5km) section that leads along a quiet minor road from Gairlochy to Clunes. Note that there is a busy road crossing just before Neptune's Staircase.

REFRESHMENTS
- Lots of choice in Fort William.
- Cafe barge, Laggan Locks.
- Great Glen Water Park, North Laggan.

Old Inverlochy Castle, Fort William

Caledonian Canal

THINGS TO SEE & DO

- **Glen Nevis Visitor Centre:** whether you want to scale Ben Nevis or learn about its geology and history, the centre will provide you with an enjoyable and informative look at the mountain; information is also available on other fine walks through the glen; 01397 705922; www.highland.gov.uk
- **Nevis Range mountain bike trails:** see Nearby Cycle Routes on page 105.
- **The Ice Factor National Ice Climbing Centre, Kinlochleven:** if you want to chill for the afternoon while getting some ice climbing in, this is the place; 01855 831100; www.ice-factor.co.uk

TRAIN STATIONS

Fort William; Banavie; Corpach.

BIKE HIRE

- **Alpine Bikes, Fort William:** 01397 704008; www.alpinebikes.com
- **Nevis Cycles, Inverlochy, Fort William:** 01397 705555; www.neviscycles.com

FURTHER INFORMATION

- To view or print National Cycle Network routes, visit www.sustrans.org.uk
- Maps and leaflets for this area are available from www.sustransshop.co.uk
- For further information on routes in Scotland, visit www.routes2ride.org.uk/scotland
- For details on local routes, visit www.ridefortwilliam.co.uk
- For details on the full range of activities available in Fort William, visit

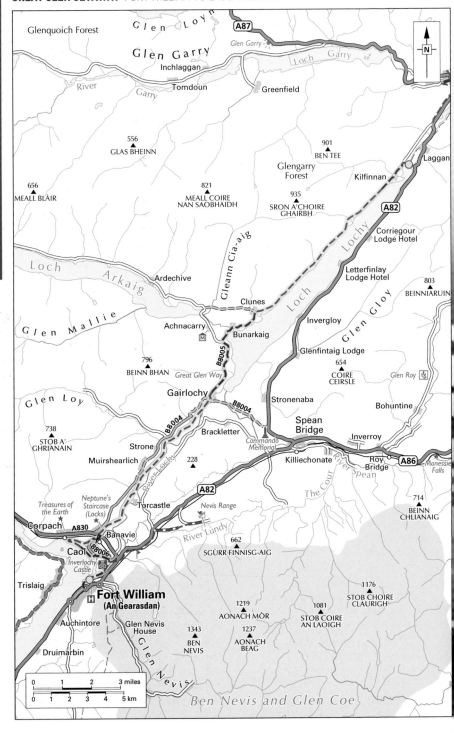

Glenquoich Forest

Glen Loyn

A87

Glen Garry

Glen Garry

Loch Garry

Inchlaggan

River Garry

Tomdoun

Greenfield

556
GLAS BHEINN

901
BEN TEE

Glengarry
Forest

Kilfinnan

Laggan

656
MEALL BLÀIR

821
MEALL COIRE
NAN SAOBHAIDH

935
SRON A'CHOIRE
GHAIRBH

A82

Corriegour
Lodge Hotel

Loch Arkaig

Ardechive

Gleann Cia-aig

Loch Lochy

Letterfinlay
Lodge Hotel

Clunes

803
BEINNIARUIN

Glen Mallie

Achnacarry

Bunarkaig

Invergloy

Glen Gloy

Glenfintaig Lodge

796
BEINN BHAN

B8005

Great Glen Way

654
COIRE
CEIRSLE

Glen Roy

Glen Loy

Gairlochy

B8004

Stronenaba

Spean
Bridge

Bohuntine

738
STOB A'
GHRIANAIN

B8004

Brackletter

Commando
Memorial

Inverroy

Strone

River Lochy

228

Killiechonate

Roy
Bridge

A86

Monessie
Falls

Muirshearlich

River Spean

The Cour

714
BEINN
CHLIANAIG

Neptune's
Staircase
(Locks)

Torcastle

A82

Nevis Range

Treasures of
the Earth

Corpach

A830

Banavie

River Lundy

662
SGÙRR FINNISG-AIG

Caol

B8006

1176
STOB CHOIRE
CLAURIGH

Inverlochy
Castle

Trislaig

**Fort William
(An Gearasdan)**

1219
AONACH MÒR

1081
STOB COIRE
AN LAOIGH

Auchintore

Glen Nevis
House

1343
BEN
NEVIS

1237
AONACH
BEAG

Druimarbin

Glen Nevis

Ben Nevis and Glen Coe

0   1   2   3 miles
0   1   2   3   4   5 km

Neptune's Staircase on the Caledonian Canal

www.outdoorcapital.co.uk
- Highlands Tourist Information: 0845 225 5121; 0131 625 8625; www.visithighlands.com
- Scotland Tourist Information: 0845 225 5121; 0131 625 8625; www.visitscotland.com

ROUTE DESCRIPTION
Follow the Great Glen Way signs and thistle waymarkers from the train station along both on-road and traffic-free cyclepaths to reach the Caledonian Canal. Cycle along the towpath to Gairlochy and then join the minor road to Clunes. From there, follow the Great Glen Way signs to pedal by long Loch Lochy on a stony track to Laggan Locks. The recently upgraded towpath continues north for 1.5 miles (2.5km).

NEARBY CYCLE ROUTES
The Fort William to Laggan Locks trail is part of a longer route that continues for a further 11 miles (17.5km) to Fort Augustus. The Fort William to Fort Augustus trail will become part of National Route 78, which will extend from Inverness to Campbeltown; the 120-mile (193km) Oban to Campbeltown section is in place, as are sections between Ganavan and Dunbeg, the Sea Life Sanctuary and Dalnatrat,

and Ballachulish and Kentallen. There is also a section of quiet road heading up from North Connel and a cycle track in Duror.

A family-friendly section of the Caledonian Canal runs from Bridge of Oich to Fort Augustus. This 5-mile (8km) scenic towpath through the Great Glen emerges by a flight of locks and leads through town to Loch Ness.

Nevis Range offers world-class mountain bike trails and has one to suit every level of rider. The trails, at Torlundy near Fort William, can be accessed by a traffic-free cyclepath from the Fort William to Laggan Locks trail at Inverlochy Castle.

CAIRNGORM GLORY – AVIEMORE TO CARRBRIDGE

Get away from it all on the marvellous Route 7 through the Cairngorms National Park. Almost entirely traffic-free, the ride follows good tracks and cyclepaths, allowing you to focus on the majesty of the surroundings.

From Aviemore, the route climbs briefly through woods to reach open, heather-filled country. Dense stands of lichen-clad silver birch add incredible colour in the autumn, while the deep corries of the high northern Cairngorms draw the eye. In the summer months, you'll see the Strathspey steam train pass by, filling the air with the sights and sounds of yesteryear.

From Boat of Garten, a delightful, level cyclepath leads to a hillier off-road section, which delves into a pine forest to emerge at Carrbridge. The quaint village boasts an attractive, narrow, arched stone bridge, which dates back to 1717. Known locally as 'the coffin bridge', it was used by funeral parties to reach Duthil Churchyard.

From Carrbridge, a recommended option is to pedal on, past the train station, to Slochd. A fine off-road variant, also on Route 7, can be followed through pine and birch woods to Sluggan Bridge. Built in the 1830s for General Wade's military road, it was restored by Sustrans in 2002. On the far side of the River Dulnain, the track leads through Scots pines to 406m (1,320ft) high Slochd Summit.

ROUTE INFORMATION
National Route: 7
Start: Aviemore train station.
Finish: Carrbridge train station.
Distance: 11 miles (17.5km).

Grade: Moderate.
Surface: Tarmac and off-road track.
Hills: Small hill as you leave Aviemore; stiff but short climb as you begin the off-road section after Boat of Garten.

Red squirrel at Boat of Garten

YOUNG & INEXPERIENCED CYCLISTS
This is ideal for novice cyclists and older children, though great care should be taken crossing the A95. The Aviemore-Boat of Garten section is best for younger children, but those under 8 might struggle with the rough surface.

REFRESHMENTS
- Lots of choice in Aviemore.
- Anderson's Restaurant, Boat of Garten.
- The Old Bakery, Carrbridge.
- Cairn Hotel, Carrbridge.

THINGS TO SEE & DO
- Strathspey Steam Railway: atmospheric train ride from Aviemore to Boat of Garten, with views of the Cairngorms; cycles carried; 01479 810725; www.strathspeyrailway.co.uk
- Loch Garten RSPB Visitor Centre, near Boat

The River Spey at Boat of Garten

of Garten: one of the best places in the UK to see ospreys and capercaillies; access from Route 7; 01479 831476; www.rspb.org.uk

- **Landmark Forest Adventure Park, Carrbridge:** adventure playground with a tree-top trail, water slides and educational exhibitions; 0800 731 3446; www.landmarkpark.co.uk
- **Tomatin Distillery, Tomatin:** a whisky still has bubbled here since the 15th century; guided tours available of this fabled distillery on the River Findhorn; 01463 248148; www.tomatin.com
- **Cairngorm Reindeer Herd, Glenmore, near Aviemore:** see Britain's only herd of wild reindeer, reintroduced to the Cairngorms in the 1950s; 01479 861228; www.reindeer-company.demon.co.uk

TRAIN STATIONS
Aviemore; Carrbridge. Note that the service between these stations is limited and bikes must be pre-booked.

BIKE HIRE
- **Mikes Bikes, Aviemore:** 01479 810478; www.aviemorebikes.co.uk
- **Bothy Bikes, Inverdruie:** 01479 810111; www.bothybikes.co.uk

FURTHER INFORMATION
- To view or print National Cycle Network routes, visit www.sustrans.org.uk
- Maps for this area are available to buy from www.sustransshop.co.uk
- For further information on routes in Scotland, visit

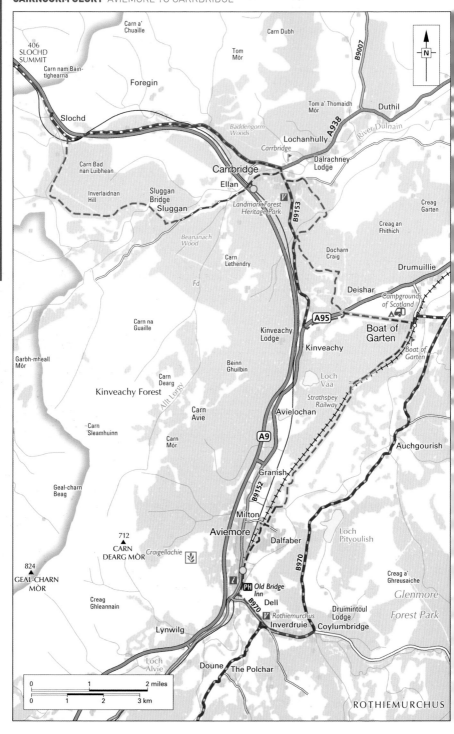

www.routes2ride.org.uk/scotland
- The Cairngorms National Park Authority: 01479 873535; www.cairngorms.co.uk
- Aviemore Tourist Information: 01479 810200; http://visitcairngorms.com
- Scotland Tourist Information: 0845 225 5121; 0131 625 8625; www.visitscotland.com

ROUTE DESCRIPTION

This route follows off-road variants on Route 7. The section to Boat of Garten can be accessed from the southbound platform of Aviemore train station. Alternatively, cycle left down the High Street from the station to follow a Route 7-signed ramp. Turn left at the bottom.

The off-road track leads for 5 miles (8km) to Boat of Garten. During the summer season, you could catch the Strathspey steam train back to the start from here – an experience that little ones will love.

The ride continues, following Route 7 northbound signs for Inverness, along a dedicated cyclepath that runs beside a road but is blissfully separated from it by a grassy buffer – a paragon of cycleway design.

After approximately 1 mile (1.6km), at the junction with the A95, this route follows the second off-road variant: cross the A-road with great care to follow the minor road to Docharn. There is a fairly steep though short climb here, but it's worth it for the superb views of the Cairngorms and Strathspey. The track ends in Carrbridge. To return by train (pre-booking of bike space essential), follow Route 7 off-road signs by the old bridge to access the station.

To continue to Slochd Summit, on a superb off-road track, simply follow the Route 7 signs past the station for 5 miles (8km).

NEARBY CYCLE ROUTES

The Aviemore to Carrbridge trail is part of the 429-mile (690km) Lochs & Glens Cycle Route (National Route 7), which runs from Carlisle to Inverness. The Old Logging Trail – a surfaced traffic-free trail – can be followed from

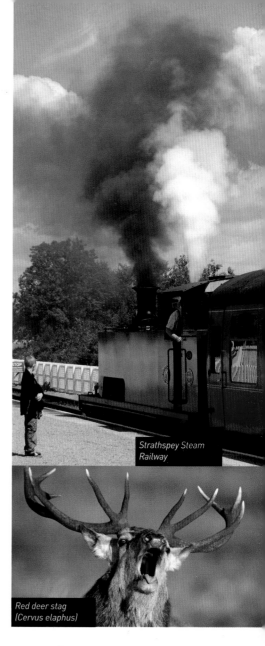

Strathspey Steam Railway

Red deer stag (Cervus elaphus)

Inverdruie (on Route 7) to Glenmore and Loch Morlich. It is ideal for families and provides good views.

The Rothiemurchus Estate by Aviemore has a range of excellent family-friendly off-road cycle trails. Among them is a circuit of Loch an Eilein.

HIGHLAND FLING – INVERNESS TO DINGWALL

Inverness, set at the mouth of the River Ness, the terminal of the Caledonian Canal and the junction of the Beauly Firth with the Moray Firth, is known as the capital of the Highlands. It is by some distance the largest settlement in the Highlands and lies at a junction of two National Cycle Network routes: Route 1 passes through the town on its way from Aberdeen to John o'Groats and it is also the terminus of Route 7, the Lochs & Glens Route, which starts in Carlisle. In the future, Route 78, with a starting point at Campbeltown on the Mull of Kintyre, will follow the Great Glen to finish at Inverness.

The route to Dingwall crosses the A9 Kessock Bridge on a cyclepath and passes beneath the Iron Age hill fort on Ord Hill on the north side of Beauly Firth. Quiet lanes and a newly built cyclepath alongside the A835 to the northwest of Tore lead to the bridge built by Thomas Telford in 1809 over the River Conon at Maryburgh, at the head of Cromarty Firth. Keep an eye out here for red kites, with their distinctive forked tails, which you may see wheeling overhead. Dingwall's oldest building, a former schoolhouse, dates back to 1650. There is good birdwatching from Dingwall's harbour foreshore.

ROUTE INFORMATION
National Route: 1
Start: Ness Bridge, over the river near Inverness train station.
Finish: Dingwall town centre.
Distance: 14 miles (22.5km).
Grade: Moderate.
Surface: Tarmac.

Kessock Bridge over the Ness Estuary

Hills: Some hills, with great views over Dingwall as a result!

YOUNG & INEXPERIENCED CYCLISTS
A combination of quiet roads and cyclepaths. There are a number of access roads across the A835 cycle track and road crossings at the Tore roundabout and at Maryburgh, where care should be taken. There is a steep hill down to North Kessock.

REFRESHMENTS
- Lots of choice in Inverness and Dingwall.
- Cafe and North Kessock Hotel in North Kessock.

THINGS TO SEE & DO
- **Inverness Museum and Art Gallery:** covers the history and heritage of the capital of the Highlands; 01463 237114; www.museumsgalleriesscotland.org.uk
- **Inverness Castle:** dating from the 1830s, overlooking the River Ness; www.undiscoveredscotland.co.uk
- **Inverness Cathedral:** dating from 1866; 01463 233535; www.invernesscathedral.co.uk
- **North Kessock Dolphin and Seal Centre:** one of the best places in Europe to observe

dolphins and seals in their natural habitat; open June to September; 01463 731866; www.highland.gov.uk/leisureandtourism
• **Dingwall Museum:** local museum with pretty courtyard and picnic tables; 01349 865366; www.museumsgalleriesscotland.org.uk
• **Black Isle Brewery, Allangrange:** 1-mile (1.6km) detour off the route; small independent organic brewery; 01463 811871; www.blackislebrewery.com

TRAIN STATIONS
Inverness; Dingwall.

BIKE HIRE
• **Highland Bicycle Company, Inverness:** 01463 234789; www.highlandbikes.com
• **Ticket to Ride, Culloden Moor:** offers bike delivery; 07902 242301; www.tickettoridehighlands.co.uk

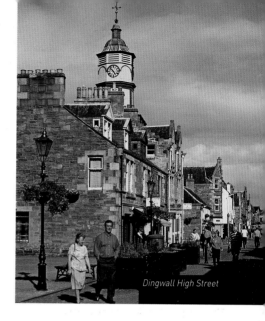
Dingwall High Street

FURTHER INFORMATION
• To view or print National Cycle Network routes, visit www.sustrans.org.uk
• Maps for this area are available to buy from www.sustransshop.co.uk
• For more information on routes in Scotland, visit www.routes2ride.org.uk/scotland
• **Inverness Tourist Information:** 01463 234353
• **Highlands Tourist Information:** www.visithighlands.com
• **Scotland Tourist Information:** 0845 225 5121; www.visitscotland.com

ROUTE DESCRIPTION
Follow Route 1 north from the centre of Inverness, along the River Ness to Kessock Bridge.

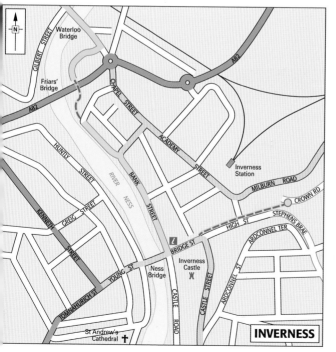

INVERNESS

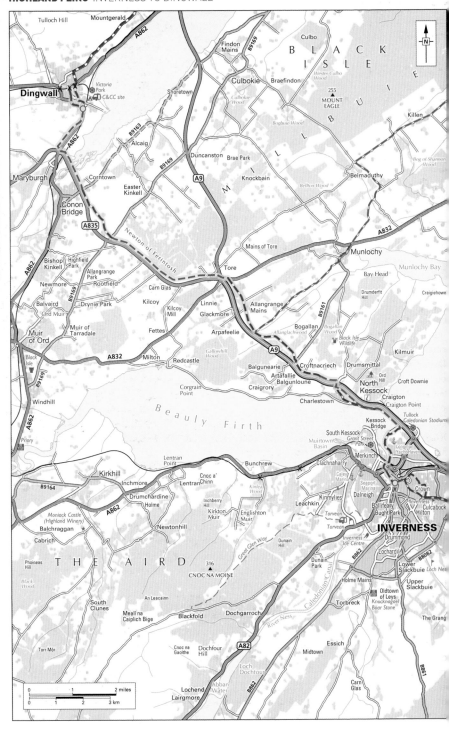

View over Dingwall

The Castle, Inverness

A cycle track on the west side of the bridge takes you over the Beauly Firth to the Black Isle – despite its name, it is not an island. As you cross the bridge, you can see the village of North Kessock far below. Once over the bridge, you have a choice of routes.

Route 1 heads down to the left, but you can continue on the cycleway alongside the A9 to reach the Tourist Information Centre and the Dolphin and Seal Centre.

To reach North Kessock, follow the signs for Route 1 down the hill and enjoy a pleasant cycle by the shore through this old village.

At the western end of the village, Route 1 heads uphill, where it rejoins the A9 cycleway and then goes under the A9 to join a cycle track for 0.5 mile (0.8km) followed by a minor road for 3.5 miles (5.5km) to Tore. As you head along the route, you'll see a sign for the Black Isle Brewery, a 1-mile (1.6km) detour from Route 1. This road also leads to the Cromarty Ferry (open in summer only) if you want to do a circuit round the Cromarty Firth.

Use the cyclepath to circumnavigate the Tore roundabout, turn sharp right through a narrow opening at the west side and pass some houses before joining a traffic-free cycle track that runs for just under 3 miles (5km) to where the route crosses the B9169. Another stretch of quiet road leads down to near Conon Bridge – red kites are frequently seen circling overhead along this section. From Conon Bridge, there's another stretch of cycle track leading over the bridge and to the roundabout at Maryburgh, where you cross the road and take a right turn along a stretch of traffic-free route, taking you almost into the centre of Dingwall.

NEARBY CYCLE ROUTES

National Route 1 heads north from Inverness to John o'Groats, and south to Aberdeen. National Route 7 heads south to Aviemore, Pitlochry and Glasgow.

The Great Glen Way is a signed, long-distance walking route west out of Inverness along Loch Ness and the Caledonian Canal to Fort William. It is best suited to mountain bikes.

DEESIDE WAY – ABERDEEN TO BANCHORY

Following the Deeside Way makes for a lovely, stress-free day out with plenty to see en route, including exceptional Crathes and Drum Castles and a recreated steam railway.

This family-friendly route, which runs from Aberdeen to Royal Deeside, mainly follows a former railway line where old steam trains used to puff and whistle. As you leave the Granite City (Aberdeen), there is information about all the former railway stations, which were in use until the mid-1960s, as well as views of the impressive River Dee through the trees. Abandoned platforms, and other remnants of the ghost stations, can be seen as you pedal along.

The route follows the line as far as Banchory – a manageable amount for a day out, though fitter cyclists could continue to the terminus at Ballater. Originally, in the 1840s, the engineers planned that the line would continue further west to Braemar, but Queen Victoria explained, in no uncertain terms, that she didn't want the railway drawing the hordes close to her Balmoral residence.

This a nice cycle ride at any time of year but it perhaps comes into its own in the autumn, when the sheltered nature of the railway line means you can avoid much of the gusty weather, and the sides of the track blaze with colour.

ROUTE INFORMATION
National Route: 195
Start: Aberdeen train station.
Finish: Banchory town centre.
Distance: 19 miles (30.5km).
Grade: Easy.
Surface: First 5 miles (8km) tarmac, then dust; can be muddy in places.
Hills: Some hills on the link route from Aberdeen station to Duthie Park. From there, it's just a gentle upwards incline.

YOUNG & INEXPERIENCED CYCLISTS
Ideal for all cyclists, though see Route Description on page 117 for further information.

REFRESHMENTS
- Lots of choice in Aberdeen.
- Cafe and pub in Peterculter.
- Crathes Castle cafe, near Banchory.
- Lots of choice in Banchory.

THINGS TO SEE & DO
- Old Aberdeen: the cobbled streets of Old Aberdeen, once a separate burgh, are lined with historic buildings mainly dating back to

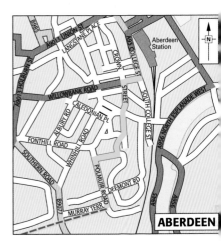

ABERDEEN

the 17th and 18th centuries; the 15th-century court and chapel of Aberdeen University's King's College are of particular note; 01224 288828; www.aberdeen-grampian.com
- Aberdeen Maritime Museum, Shiprow: learn about Aberdeen's links with the sea, from the oil industry through the port's long history of fishing and shipbuilding; models and computer animation bring the experience to

Daffodils by Riverside Road, Aberdeen

Holburn Bridge on the Deeside Way

life; 01224 337700; www.aagm.co.uk
- **Duthie Park, Aberdeen:** the Winter Gardens house many exotic plants, including the largest collection of cacti in Britain; boating on the ponds is also available; 01224 523292; www.aberdeencity.gov.uk
- **Crathes Castle, near Banchory:** one of the most beautiful and best-preserved castles in Scotland, occupied by the Burnetts of Leys for over 350 years and set against a magnificent garden; its June flower border is world-renowned; 0844 493 2166; www.nts.org.uk

TRAIN STATIONS
Aberdeen.

BIKE HIRE
- **Foundry Bike Co, Aberdeen:** 01224 642020; www.foundrybikes.co.uk

FURTHER INFORMATION
- To view or print National Cycle Network routes, visit www.sustrans.org.uk
- Maps for this area are available to buy from www.sustransshop.co.uk
- For further information on routes in Scotland, visit www.routes2ride.org.uk/scotland
- **Aberdeen City and Shire Tourist Information:** 01224 288828; www.aberdeen-grampian.com
- **Scotland Tourist Information:** 0845 225 5121; 0131 625 8625; www.visitscotland.com

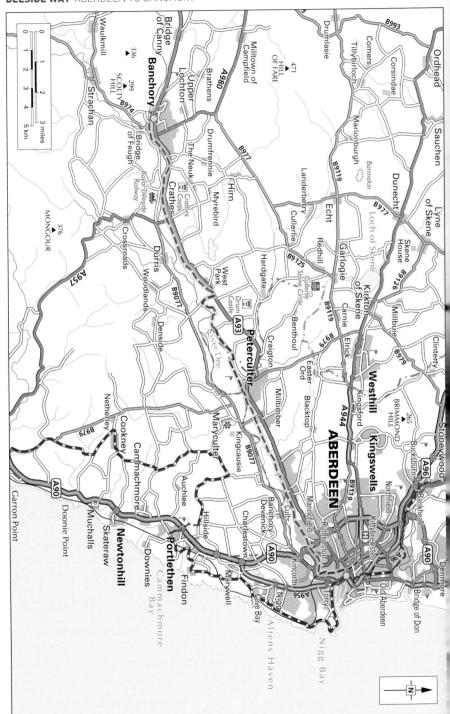

Crathes Castle and gardens

ROUTE DESCRIPTION

See the insert map for the link from Aberdeen train station to Duthie Park. This mile-long (1.6km) section follows busy roads from the train station to a residential area. Inexperienced cyclists could walk the link on footpaths.

At Duthie Park, the Deeside Way is accessed through the car park to the right of the north entrance. From there it's very easy to follow – just go straight. Note, especially if there are children with you, that the Way is intersected by several unannounced roads.

Heading west out of Peterculter, there is a short on-road section followed by a very rough and narrow section of track (you may prefer to use the road) and shortly afterwards by an on-road section for a mile (1.6km).

At Drumoak and Crathes, the route runs alongside the A93 for short distances. Use the footways and take great care if crossing the road. Apart from this, the route continues along the railway line, past the steam railway at Milton, where the path can be muddy. The path ends in a public park in Banchory, where this section of the cyclepath ends.

NEARBY CYCLE ROUTES

The Deeside Way trail from Aberdeen to Banchory is part of the longer Deeside Way (National Route 195). The route is complete further west, where it follows the old railway line from Aboyne to Ballater. The section between Banchory and Aboyne will eventually follow forest roads, minor roads and paths. Currently you can ride to Aboyne on trails through Blackhall Forest and minor roads.

In Aberdeen, you can take National Route 1 north to John o'Groats, through wild and awesome landscapes, or south to Edinburgh and Newcastle on the Coast & Castles Route.

Kirkhill Forest, to the northwest of Aberdeen, has family-friendly forest trails and a mile-long (1.6km) stretch of mountain bike fun park.

Blackhall Forest overlooks the River Dee near Banchory and includes Scolty Woodland Park, a popular, well-marked mountain trail. Scolty Hill, with its monument at the top, is a well-known landmark with views for miles. When complete, the Deeside Way will use a route through this forest and then minor roads to Potarch.

FORMARTINE & BUCHAN WAY – DYCE TO ELLON

Enjoy cycling along this flat, traffic-free route. Although the track can be rough in places, it's particularly attractive in the warmer months, when the hedgerows come alive and you can enjoy views across this rich, northeast farmland.

The Formartine & Buchan Way tracks the path of an old railway line. The route follows the Way from Dyce (its southernmost point) and travels north, past the villages of Newmachar and Udny Station (now only a station in name), to finish in the attractive town of Ellon on the wildlife-rich River Ythan. The Dyce to Newmachar section is shared with National Route 1.

Dating back to 1861, the Formartine & Buchan Railway took its name from the districts through which it passed, with Formartine lying between the River Don and the River Ythan, and Buchan lying between the River Ythan and the River Deveron.

The Way, as a whole, offers great cycling. From Dyce, it leads for 25 miles (40km) through the heart of rural Aberdeenshire to Maud, where it splits. It then continues north for 15 miles (24km) to Fraserburgh, while cycling east will take you to Peterhead – an easy 13 miles (21km) from Maud. The Way also passes through (or close to) many places of interest, including Aden Country Park and Drinnies Wood Observatory.

ROUTE INFORMATION
National Route: 1 (to Newmachar)
Start: Dyce train station.
Finish: Ellon town centre.
Distance: 13 miles (21km).
Grade: Easy.
Surface: Track, but becomes rougher between Newmachar and Udny Station.
Hills: None.

YOUNG & INEXPERIENCED CYCLISTS
More suited to older children and confident novices due to rough surface in places. Children should cycle behind adults due to unannounced road crossings where railway crossings have been removed.

REFRESHMENTS
• Lots of choice in Dyce.
• Udny Station Hotel, with beer garden.
• Lots of choice in Ellon.

THINGS TO SEE & DO
• Old Aberdeen: the cobbled streets of Old Aberdeen, once a separate burgh, are lined with historic buildings mainly dating back to the 17th and 18th centuries; the 15th-century court and chapel of Aberdeen University's King's College stand out among many fine buildings; 01224 288828; www.aberdeen-grampian.com
• Aberdeen Maritime Museum, Shiprow: learn about Aberdeen's links with the sea, from the oil industry through the port's long history of fishing and shipbuilding; models and computer animation bring the experience to life; 01224 337700; www.aagm.co.uk
• Pitmedden Garden, Ellon: features more than 5 miles (8km) of box hedging arranged in intricate patterns to form six parterres; particularly colourful in the summer months; each parterre is filled with some 40,000 plants; 0844 493 2177; www.nts.org.uk
• Tolquhon Castle, near Pitmedden: noted for its highly ornamented gatehouse; the castle also has a secret hiding-place – a compartment below the floor in the laird's bedchamber on the second floor, where Sir William hid his valuables; 01651 851286; www.historic-scotland.gov.uk

*Parterre in
Pitmedden Garden*

TRAIN STATIONS
Dyce.

BIKE HIRE
- Foundry Bike Co, Aberdeen: 01224 642020;
  www.foundrybikes.co.uk

FURTHER INFORMATION
- To view or print National Cycle Network
  routes, visit www.sustrans.org.uk
- Maps for this area are available to buy from
  www.sustransshop.co.uk
- For further information on routes in Scotland,
  visit www.routes2ride.org.uk/scotland
- Aberdeen City and Shire Tourist Information:
  01224 288828; www.aberdeen-grampian.com
- Scotland Tourist Information: 0845 225 5121;
  0131 625 8625; www.visitscotland.com

ROUTE DESCRIPTION
This route, following a linear section of railway,
should present few navigational problems, and
it can be easily accessed from Dyce train
station. From the eastern platform, simply
follow the road north to reach a track. The way

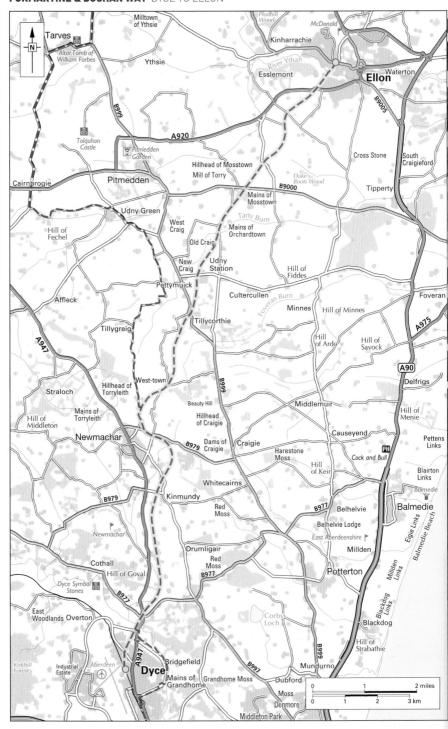

is also signed with Route 1 signs as far as Newmachar, where Route 1 turns northwest on minor roads towards Udny Green. Continue on the railway path to Udny Station and Ellon. Be prepared for some slow cycling, as the route is quite rough and prone to waterlogging in places. Skinny-tyred bicycles will struggle – hybrid or mountain bikes are recommended.

If you are travelling beyond Ellon on the Formartine & Buchan Way, note that there is currently a section between Maud and Brucklay Bridge that is unsurfaced. A diversion is in place using the B9106 and A950. This is unsuitable for inexperienced cyclists and young children.

NEARBY CYCLE ROUTES

The Dyce to Ellon trail described here is part of the longer bifurcate Formartine & Buchan Way, which extends from Dyce to Fraserburgh and Peterhead.

The Dyce to Ellon/Formartine & Buchan Way trail shares the Dyce to Newmachar section with National Route 1. This extends north to John o'Groats and south to Aberdeen, Edinburgh and Newcastle.

The North Sea Cycle Route follows National Route 1 along the east coast of Scotland and through the Shetlands and Orkneys. This 3,750-mile (6,000km) route passes through eight countries bordering the North Sea (www.northsea-cycle.com).

Kirkhill Forest, to the northwest of Aberdeen, has forest trails that are ideal for family cycling, as well as a mile-long (1.6km) stretch of mountain bike fun park.

Tolquhon Castle courtyard

MORAY DELIGHT – CULLEN TO GARMOUTH

This coastal route is one that all the family and novice riders can enjoy. More experienced riders will also appreciate the thrill that always accompanies a cycle ride by the sea. For the most part, the route hugs the Moray coast, where there are many opportunities to stop and explore the varied shoreline. It's also worth taking time to soak up the atmosphere in the tight-knit fishing villages, such as Portknockie and Findochty (pronounced Finechty), which the ride passes through.

The trip starts dramatically in Cullen as National Route 1 leads steeply down to join an old railway, crossing over two viaducts, with fine views of Cullen Bay. In Portknockie, a short detour is worth taking to the Bow Fiddle Rock, a wave-crafted sea arch.

The same disused railway line provides an easy approach to Buckie, where, on a good day, there are extensive views across the Moray Firth to the hills of Sutherland and Caithness. Further on, the route crosses the River Spey on the Spey Bay Viaduct, which once carried trains across this mighty river of the north.

Garmouth, the finish point, is easily reached. However, it's a good idea to take a detour to both sides of the Spey mouth. On the east, there is a wildlife centre, with the chance to see large pods of dolphins; on the west side, you can pedal along to Kingston, where there's a long shingle beach.

ROUTE INFORMATION
National Route: 1
Start: North Deskford Street, Cullen.
Finish: Garmouth village centre.
Distance: 14 miles (22.5km).
Grade: Easy to moderate.
Surface: Tarmac, stone dust.
Hills: Mainly flat or undulating; no major climbs.

YOUNG & INEXPERIENCED CYCLISTS
Most of the route is ideal for novices and families with young children, as long as care is taken on the quiet road sections. On the busier sections, through the centre of Buckie and along the A990 west of Buckie, they should dismount and walk along the pavement.

REFRESHMENTS
• Plenty of choice along the route.
• Pub and hotel in Garmouth.

THINGS TO SEE & DO

- **Bow Fiddle Rock, Portknockie:** lying just off the coast at Portknockie, this character-filled sea arch looks like the bow of a fiddle; a much-loved local landmark.
- **Buckie and District Fishing Heritage Centre:** houses an extensive photographic collection, as well as numerous artefacts relating to the area's fishing tradition; www.buckieheritage.org
- **Scottish Dolphin Centre, Spey Bay:** the Whale and Dolphin Conservation Society (WDCS), based on the southern shore of the Moray Firth, is the perfect place to find out about the amazing wildlife of this area, including bottlenose dolphins; 01343 820339; www.wdcs.org
- **Tugnet Ice House, Spey Bay:** huge 19th-century ice house that was once integral to a salmon-fishing station before the prized fish were shipped south to market.

TRAIN STATIONS

Elgin.

BIKE HIRE

- **Rafford Cycles, Forres:** 01309 672811; http://myweb.tiscali.co.uk/recycles

FURTHER INFORMATION

- To view or print National Cycle Network routes, visit www.sustrans.org.uk
- Maps for this area are available to buy from www.sustransshop.co.uk
- For further information on routes in Scotland, visit www.routes2ride.org.uk/scotland
- **Banff Tourist Information:** 01261 812419

Bow Fiddle Rock near Portknockie

Cycling over Cullen viaduct

Dolphins at play at Moray Firth

final section of railway path, crossing the Spey Bay Viaduct to arrive in Garmouth.

NEARBY CYCLE ROUTES

The Cullen to Garmouth trail is part of the 500-mile (804km) Aberdeen to John o'Groats route (National Route 1). This is also part of the North Sea Cycle Route, a 3,750-mile (6,000km) route that passes through eight countries bordering the North Sea (www.northsea-cycle.com).

The Moray Monster Trails are a network of mountain-biking trails that join three distinct centres, at Whiteash and Ordiequish, both of which are by Fochabers, and at Ben Aigan, near Craigellachie. The trails cover all grades (www.forestry.gov.uk).

The Speyside Way – a famous long-distance path – is suitable for cycling between Fochabers and Ballindalloch. Other sections of the Way are less suitable, and cyclists are asked at all times to ensure that they use the route in a way that does not cause damage to the track surface, or cause inconvenience or danger to users on foot or horseback (www.speysideway.org).

From Portgordon, you can follow the off-road Speyside Way via Lower Auchenreath to the B9104 by the Spey mouth.

• Scotland Tourist Information: 0845 225 5121; 0131 625 8625; www.visitscotland.com

ROUTE DESCRIPTION

From the north end of Cullen's North Deskford Street, join National Route 1 to cycle along an old railway line and over two spectacular viaducts.

After a short stretch, along the quiet streets of Portknockie, the route joins the coastal path to Findochty. From there the route crosses the A942 to follow a railway path for 2.5 miles (4km) into Buckie.

A level A-road leads out of Buckie, along by the coast, before the route rejoins the railway track to Portgordon. Further on, after a series of minor roads, the route follows a delightful

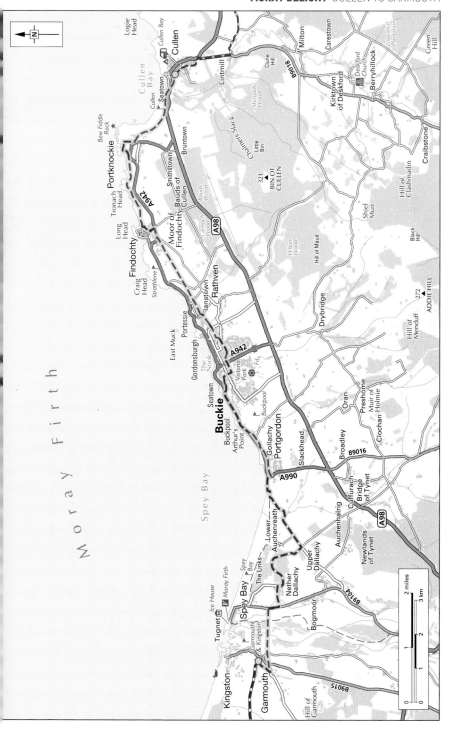

NEXT STEPS...

We hope you have enjoyed the cycle rides in this book.

Sustrans developed the National Cycle Network to act as a catalyst for bringing cycling (and walking) back into our everyday lives. Between the 1950s and the mid-1970s cycling in the UK fell by 80%. Cycling now accounts for only about 2% of all journeys made in the UK, a fraction of what we used to achieve.

When you consider that nearly 6 in 10 car journeys are under 5 miles, it makes you wonder what the potential for increasing levels of cycling is. Evidence shows that, for local journeys under 5 miles, most of us could make 9 out of 10 journeys on foot, bike or public transport if there was more investment in making it possible to leave the car behind.

And why not? We can all be more savvy when it comes to travel. One small step becomes one giant leap if we all start walking away from less healthy lifestyles and pedalling our way towards happier children and a low carbon world.

And that's where Sustrans comes in. Sustainable travel means carbon-reducing, energy-efficient, calorie-burning, money-saving travel. Here are a few things that we think make sense. If you agree, join us.

- **Snail's pace** – 20mph or less on our streets where we live, go to school, shop and work – make it the norm, not just when there's snow or ice on the roads.

- **Closer encounters** – planning that focuses on good non-motorised access, so that we can reach more post offices, schools, shops, doctors and dentists without the car.

- **People spaces** – streets where kids can play hopscotch or football and be free-range, and where neighbours can meet and chat, and safe, local walking and cycling routes, to school and beyond.

- **Road revolution** – build miles and miles of bike paths that don't evaporate when they meet a road.

- **Find our feet** – campaign for pedestrian-friendly city centres, or wide boulevards with regular pedestrian crossings and slow-moving traffic.

- **Better buses** – used by millions, under-invested by billions and, if affordable, reliable and pleasant to use, could make local car journeys redundant.

- **More car clubs** – a car club on every street corner and several for every new-build estate.

- **Rewards for car-sharing** – get four in a car and take more than half the cars off the road.

- **Trains** – more of them, and cheaper.

- **Become a staycationer** – and holiday at home. Mountains, beaches, culture, great beer, good food and a National Cycle Network that connects them all.

If we work towards these goals we have a chance of delivering our fair share of the 80% reduction in CO_2 by mid-century that we're now committed to by law, and some of the 100% reduction that many climate experts now consider essential.

To find out more and join the movement, visit www.sustrans.org.uk

Free. Clean. Green.

Photo: Rita Platts/ Sustrans

Few people would say that they don't care about the environment, don't want to get fit or don't care about the damage pollution is doing to local communities – but what's the answer? The humble bike: a great way to get from A to B, cut carbon emissions and get fit at the same time. The bike is the greenest machine on the road, and Sustrans is doing everything it can to help people cycle more. Sustrans developed the National Cycle Network to help bring cycling (and walking) back into everyday life.

Cycling only accounts for 2% of all the journeys made in the UK today.
90% of all journeys under five miles could be made by foot, public transport or bike. And we are trying to do everything possible to make this happen.
Help us provide everyone with a greener way to travel.

If you care about the environment and love cycling, you should support Sustrans. Get online at sustrans.org.uk, join the movement and find out how Sustrans can improve your cycling experience.

sustrans

JOIN THE MOVEMENT

ACKNOWLEDGEMENTS

The Automobile Association would like to thank the following photographers, companies and picture libraries for their assistance in the preparation of this book.

Abbreviations for the picture credits are as follows – (t) top; (b) bottom; (l) left; (r) right; (c) centre; (dps) double page spread; (AA) AA World Travel Library

Front cover: View of Loch Lomond from the top of Conic Hill; AA/Steve Day.
Back cover: David Byrne, Danny Clinch.

3bl Jon Bewley/Sustrans; 3br AA/Jeff Beazley; 4 Danny Clinch; 5c AA/Mark Hamblin; 5bl AA/Stephen Whitehorne; 5cr AA/Jonathan Smith; 5br AA/Mark Hamblin; 6/7l AA/Steve Day ; 7tr AA/Ronnie Weir; 7cr AA/Ken Paterson; 7b AA/Steve Day; 11tl Jon Bewley/Sustrans; 11tr Jon Bewley/Sustrans; 11c Jon Bewley/Sustrans; 11bc Andy Huntley/Sustrans; 11br Pru Comben/Sustrans; 13t Jon Bewley/Sustrans; 13c Nicola Jones/Sustrans; 13b Jon Bewley/Sustrans; 15 AA/Karl Blackwell; 17t AA/AA; 17cr AA/Karl Blackwell; 17b Paul Hilton/Sustrans; 19 AA/Jonathan Smith; 20 AA/Ken Paterson; 22 AA/Karl Blackwell; 23t AA/Karl Blackwell; 23cr Paul Kirkwood/Sustrans; 25 Keith Brame/Sustrans; 27 AA/AA; 29t AA/Karl Blackwell; 29cr AA/Karl Blackwell; 30-31 Tom Gilland; 33 David Robertson/Alamy; 34 AA/Jonathan Smith; 35t AA/Jonathan Smith; 35b David Buchanan/Sustrans; 37 Fergal MacErlean; 38 AA/Karl Blackwell; 39t AA/Karl Blackwell; 39c AA/Karl Blackwell; 41 AA/M Alexander; 41c AA/Sue Anderson; 42bl Courtesy Chandra Prasad/Sustrans; 43t Billy Currie Photography/Getty; 45 Findlay/Alamy; 46 Courtesy Sustrans; 47 John McKenna/Alamy; 49t Phil Seale/Alamy; 51t D.G.Farquhar/Alamy; 51c Annette Price H2O

Photography/Alamy; 53 AA/Jonathan Smith; 54 ALAN OLIVER/Alamy; 55 John McKenna/Alamy; 56-57 Fergal MacErlean; 59t Kenny Williamson/Alamy; 59cr John Grimshaw/Sustrans; 61tl Arron Barnes/Alamy; 61tr John Grimshaw/Sustrans; 61c John Grimshaw/Sustrans; 63 AA/Ken Paterson; 67 Gistimages/Alamy; 69 AA/Jonathan Smith; 71 Scottish Viewpoint/Alamy; 73 BCS/Alamy; 74-75 Steve Day; 77t AA/David W Robertson; 77c AA/David W Robertson; 78 AA/David W Robertson; 79 AA/David W Robertson; 81 Jenny Baker/Sustrans; 83t AA/Jonathan Smith; 83c AA/Jonathan Smith; 85 AA/Jonathan Smith; 87 AA/Jonathan Smith; 89t AA/Jonathan Smith; 90bl Courtesy Tom Bishop/Sustrans; 91b Courtesy Tom Bishop/Sustrans; 92tl AA/Derek Forss; 95t Lynne Evans/Alamy; 95b Nick Cotton/Sustrans; 96-97 AA/Sue Anderson; 98 AA/AA; 99 AA/Sue Anderson; 100 AA/Sue Anderson; 102 Rob Ford/Alamy; 103 AA/Stephen Whitehorne; 105t AA/Steve Day; 105c Navin Mistry/Alamy; 106 AA/Jonathan Smith; 107 AA/Jonathan Smith; 109t AA/Jonathan Smith; 109b AA/Mark Hamblin; 110 AA/Eric Ellington; 111 AA/Stephen Whitehorne; 113t AA/Stephen Whitehorne; 113c AA/Jonathan Smith; 115t Jim Henderson/Alamy; 115b David Gold/Sustrans; 117 AA/Ronnie Weir; 119t David Robertson/Alamy; 119b Jon Bewley/Sustrans; 121 Mic Walker/Alamy; 122-123 Robert Harding Picture Library Ltd/Alamy; 124t Julia Bayne/Sustrans; 124c David Chapman/Alamy; 127 Courtesy Sustrans; 128 Cass Gilbert/Sustrans

Every effort has been made to trace the copyright holders, and we apologise in advance for any unintentional omissions or errors. We would be pleased to apply any corrections in the following edition of this publication.

NATIONAL CYCLE NETWORK

Go traffic-free in Scotland!

A series of four free booklets published by Sustrans describing cycle rides in Scotland:

- **NCN Edinburgh, Fife, Central & Borders**
- **NCN Glasgow & Ayrshire**
- **NCN The Central Highlands, Argyll & The Trossachs**
- **NCN Firth of Tay to Moray**

Available from **www.sustransshop.co.uk**